The Accidental Salesperson

The Accidental Salesperson

How to Take Control of Your Sales Career and Earn the Respect and Income You Deserve

Chris Lytle

AMACOM
American Management Association
New York · Atlanta · Boston · Chicago · Kansas City · San Francisco · Washington, D. C.
Brussels · Mexico City · Tokyo · Toronto

Special discounts on bulk quantities of AMACOM books are available to corporations, professional associations, and other organizations. For details, contact Special Sales Department, AMACOM, a division of American Management Association, 1601 Broadway, New York, NY 10019.
Tel.: 212-903-8316   Fax: 212-903-8083

This publication is designed to provide accurate and authoritative information in regard to the subject matter covered. It is sold with the understanding that the publisher is not engaged in rendering legal, accounting, or other professional service. If legal advice or other expert assistance is required, the services of a competent professional person should be sought.

Library of Congress Cataloging-in-Publication Data

Lytle, Chris.
    The accidental salesperson : how to take control of your sales career and earn the respect and income you deserve / Chris Lytle.
        p.   cm.
    Includes bibliographical references and index.
    ISBN 0-8144-7083-1
        1. Selling.   2. Success in business.   I. Title.
    HF5438.25 .L93   2000
    658.85—dc21   00-038092

Printing number

10   9   8   7   6   5   4   3   2   1

Contents

Introduction

Do You Believe In Destiny?

It is no accident you picked up this book. You may not have chosen sales as a profession; it may have chosen you. That applies to most of us. It is why *The Accidental Salesperson* title struck a responsive chord with you. You "ended up" in sales instead of planning this career. Now your success depends on your ability to sell your ideas, concepts, processes, and products to others—to sell on purpose, even if you ended up in sales accidentally.

You bring a lifetime of experience to this book. You already have gained plenty of wisdom about what works and what doesn't work in selling. This book will reinforce everything you are doing right. It will gently correct your course where you are off track.

You will quickly internalize the principles of selling on purpose. That's a promise. You won't have to compromise your values or change your personality to benefit. Having a new framework to think about what you do gives you a powerful edge over those accidental salespeople who have yet to embrace a philosophy of selling.

This is not a sales book for dummies. Far from it. It's a book for thinking people who realize they must sell **more** and who want to understand what works in sales today and why it works. Best of all, there are no tricks, techniques, or high-pressure tactics to learn. With a few subtle but powerful refinements in the things you're already doing, your sales will soar. This is a "why to" book filled with principles that work over and over again in selling.

You are about to learn how to take control of the dynamics of a selling situation and leverage every client contact. Very soon, you will be relying on your extraordinary selling skills instead of the faxing skills that reactive salespeople rely on. Expect to shorten your selling cycle and slash the number of objections you have to overcome.

That's just the first three chapters.

In the remaining chapters, you will learn specific strategies for every stage of the selling process. Occasionally, you will remark to yourself, "I do that already." That's good. My challenge to you is simply to do it more often and do it on purpose.

The Accidental Salesperson is not a survival manual. It is a manifesto for pros who want to thrive in sales. It's a booster shot for propelling plateaued veterans to the next level. It's a starter kit for the recent grad who has just discovered that the best jobs out there are sales jobs.

As a professional speaker, I promise my audiences more usable information per minute than any speaker out there. Well, this book contains more usable information per chapter than anything on the market. All you have to do is read and apply the concepts to your current situation. You don't even have to finish the book before you start applying its principles. Each chapter spotlights a powerful concept that's self-contained and immediately applicable to your very next client contact.

Something Socrates said may help explain why this book will have an impact on you.

"I cannot teach anybody anything. I can only make them think." Although Socrates said it in Greek twenty-four centuries or so ago, it is still relevant.

My role is to get you to think about what you're doing and why you're doing it that way. Each chapter suggests specific refinements you can make in the way you do business.

Opportunities abound for salespeople who sell on **purpose.**

To know and not to do is not to know. Education without

action is entertainment. While I hope you enjoy the book, understand that it was written for your improvement, not your enjoyment. You can read about a concept today and apply it today. You'll get the most out of *The Accidental Salesperson* by purposefully and immediately applying the concepts.

Every prospect you meet is silently saying, "Show me that you're different."

Are you ever going to show them. (Notice there is no question mark after that last sentence.)

I don't like long good-byes nor am I fond of long introductions. You're ready to start selling on purpose. So let's get started.

The Accidental Salesperson

Part 1

The Choice...the Chart...the Challenge

Chapter 1

The Choice

It's 11:45 A.M.
A coworker walks into your office or peers over your
    cubicle and says, "I'm hungry."
"Me too. Let's go to lunch," you say.
"Where do you want to go?"
"I don't know. Where do you want to go?"
"What are you hungry for?"
"Nothing special. You decide."

Chances are you have had this conversation recently with a coworker or spouse. With so many restaurants, narrowing the choice to just one becomes a daunting task.

A comedian once joked that "people don't go to Denny's Restaurants. They end up there."

They end up there precisely because they begin without a plan. They react to the hunger pang instead of anticipating it. It doesn't occur to some people that they've been getting hungry every four hours or so of their waking lives. When they finally choose a place to eat, a long line or waiting list often confronts them. As a result, they "end up" settling for something less.

But we're still hungry, so let's get back to the restaurant—any restaurant. Have you ever watched people order? Some people summon the harried waitperson and want her to act as arbiter.

"If you were me, would you have the steak or the fish?" they'll ask, as if one or the other of these portion-controlled entrees would give them a memorable culinary experience.

"Do you like steak or fish better?" says the waitperson, who now is forced into doing a customer needs analysis to get her 15 percent "commission" out of this sale. Taken to its logical conclusion, the waitperson could be forced to make the choice for the person. "How is your cholesterol, sir? If it's over two hundred, may I strongly suggest the broiled fish?"

Meanwhile, other customers wait impatiently for their second cup of coffee and mentally deduct a few percentage points from the tip they are planning to leave.

It happens all because it is so hard for some people to make a choice—any choice!

Try this little experiment. Choose a restaurant for lunch a day in advance. Use two criteria to make your choice: (1) Choose a local favorite that is not a chain. (2) Choose a place that takes reservations. Make one. Then tell (don't ask) a customer (not a coworker) that you want to take him or her to lunch. Say, "I've made reservations and I want you to join me at 12:15 tomorrow afternoon for lunch at The Edgewater if you don't have other plans."

When you get to the restaurant, look at the menu for five seconds or ignore it altogether. Say, "I'm going to have a cup of the baked onion soup, half a club sandwich, and an iced tea with extra lemon." (Order whatever you feel like having. Just do it decisively.) Prediction: Nine times out of ten your luncheon guest will order two out of the three things you ordered just because your decisiveness is so comforting and eliminates any need to make a choice.

Choices are hard for people because they already have too many. There are too many channels on television. There are too many sizes of detergent, too many brands of mustard, too many Web sites to surf. By making choices quickly and firmly, you position yourself as a decisive, take-charge person.

In the film *Moscow on the Hudson*, Robin Williams's character is a Russian musician, Vladimir Ivanoff, who defects in Bloomingdales.[1] Later, his first visit to a supermarket proves catastrophic. Used to scarcity in his homeland, he passes out from sensory overload while trying to process which coffee to buy. Regular or decaf? Ground or beans? Can or bag? Maxwell House, Folgers, Yuban, Butternut, Eight O'Clock? For Iva-noff, the choices are paralyzing.

Some people live their whole lives the way people who end up at Denny's choose a restaurant. Comedian Paula Poundstone says that adults ask kids what they want to be when they grow up because adults are still looking for ideas. It's hard enough to choose where you're going to have lunch. Think how much harder it is to choose what you're going to do for a living. The hardest part of all is committing to the choice you've made, with all of the career options still available.

When you were a little kid, you probably didn't long for—or even imagine—a career in sales. Ask some local elementary school kids what they want to be when they grow up. You'll find more future firefighters than prospective salespeople. How many children are anxiously anticipating a career of cold calling, rejection handling, price-sensitive procurement officers, delayed flights in center seats, and ninety nights a year sleeping in different hotel rooms all next to the same ice machine?

For some of us it just sort of worked out that way.

You may have "ended up" in sales as a second or third choice when something else didn't work out. You may still be wondering if sales is right for you.

Whether you're an engineer or shop foreman, CEO or account executive, your job increasingly requires excellent sales skills. When I told my neighbor, a prominent veterinarian, I was writing a book called *The Accidental Salesperson,* he said, "I'll buy one." No matter how you got into sales, this book will show you how to sell on purpose. It will guide you through the entire selling process and show you how to move your prospects through that process without skipping any steps.

It takes an Accidental Salesperson to know one. I was an Accidental Salesperson just like you. Sales, it seems, is the final frontier for liberal arts graduates who have learned how to learn, but don't know how to **do** much else.

As a 1972 graduate with a B.A. in political science, I had

three ways to use my degree and maximize the investment
my parents had made in my education. I could go to law
school, take a job in a politician's office, or become a journal-
ist and cover the political scene.

Although my grades in school had always been great,
my score on the LSAT exam was the lowest on any standard-
ized test I had ever taken. The score barely would have qualified me to attend an unaccredited night school. I took that as
a signal that law probably wasn't right for me.

After graduation, I landed a job as a summer intern for
my congressman. There I was, two weeks out of college and
working on Capitol Hill in the Cannon House Office Building.
But instead of catching "Potomac Fever," I was appalled by
the political process as it is played out in real life. The pace is
agonizingly slow, and bills become laws by a series of com-
promises and political favors.

Having eliminated law school and a political career
within six weeks of graduating, I decided to pursue that career in journalism. Reporting on the political process I so de-
spised seemed like a good career. I would become the next
Walter Cronkite (the CBS anchor who preceded Dan Rather).

At the end of my internship, I returned to my parents'
home and began my job search. Since Newark, Ohio, did not
have a television station and I didn't have any money to
move to a big city, I figured I would start my journalism career by landing a job in the news department at the local
radio station. Then, after establishing myself in the business,
it would be a fairly simple thing to move to Columbus, Ohio,
and be a TV reporter. That would lead to local anchor on the
ten o'clock news and then to the network level.

There was only one thing standing in the way of that
master plan. The general manager at the local radio station
announced during my first interview that he already had two
newsmen.

"Chris," he said, "I could put you on as an advertising
salesman."

"But you don't understand, Mr. Pricer," I said. "I'm a political science major."

"Chris, my offer still stands."

My inner dialogue went this way: "I'll do anything to get into broadcasting—even sell." My reasoning was that, once I was in the door, I could work my way into the news department.

"I'll take it," I said.

It took two weeks for me to disabuse myself of the notion that working my way into news was a good plan. The sales manager left every afternoon around four. The news director worked some nights until eleven, covering the city council meetings. The sales manager drove a Cadillac. The news director drove a beat up Chevy Vega and constantly bemoaned his fate and income. He often berated the salespeople for making too much money. From an income and status standpoint, I learned quickly that you don't "work your way into news" in a small-market radio station.

At that point, I made "The Choice" to stay in sales. I've never looked back. That choice led to a successful career in sales, sales management, and radio station ownership. In 1983, I founded a company to train radio advertising salespeople. Today we work with family businesses and Fortune 500 companies to transform sales departments into sales forces. Selling sales training has taught me even more about selling and has afforded me the privilege of traveling several million miles and speaking to more than 100,000 salespeople. More recently, I developed a series of distance learning programs. More than 8,300 people in twenty-five countries have enrolled.

All these things happened because I made The Choice to stay in sales and become good at it.

But you know what? Even if I had ended up in law school, I still would be in sales. In a law firm, a "rainmaker" is the attorney who brings clients into the firm. An attorney who can sell is called a partner.

One day I was skiing with a friend who is a dentist. I asked him, "What is the biggest issue in dentistry today?"

"Sales," he replied. "You've got to close people on having their wisdom teeth out. You have to handle objections. You have to persuade and convince them to put up with pain, expense, and time away from work. They don't teach you sales at dental school, but they should."

He had made the choice to become a dentist and had ended up an Accidental Salesperson.

So you see, you are not alone. A lot of Accidental Salespeople have learned to sell on purpose. But first, they have had to make "The Choice."

You do too.

You make The Choice when you consciously commit to your career in selling. In doing so, you gain a sense of purpose. Being able to say, "This is what I do" with a feeling of pride and certainty sets in motion undreamed of opportunities for success. Choosing to focus on becoming an excellent salesperson is liberating precisely because it eliminates the other options you're free to pursue.

You can experience much the same feeling of liberation tonight by choosing to turn off the TV instead of flipping through channels to find something worth devoting your time to. Or, if you must watch, focus on one show to the exclusion of all the others, comfortable that you've made the right choice and don't need to zip through the channels so you won't miss anything.

By not focusing, you miss everything.

That's The Choice.

Is sales right for you? When you make The Choice consciously and commit to your sales career, you gain a new sense of purpose. Making The Choice adds new focus and makes what you do more relevant.

"Hey, I was looking for a job when I found this one" is the mantra of millions of uncommitted workers today. Here's why that mantra is costing companies billions of dollars in sales each year: Research by *Purchasing* magazine[2] found that the number two thing buyers dislike about salespeople is lack of interest or purpose. The number one thing buyers dislike about salespeople is lack of preparation. Of course, if you lack interest and purpose when you approach a prospect, why would you bother to prepare?

The power of making a commitment to your career is one of the themes of our first $2 Sales Training Video.

The going rate of sales training films these days is $595 and up, but your local video store can provide you with some valuable lessons in the form of Hollywood movies for around two bucks. One of the best lessons on making The Choice comes from the film *City Slickers,* starring Billy Crystal. Jack Palance won a Best Supporting Actor Oscar for his performance as Curly in this film.

$2 Sales Training Video
City Slickers[3]

Billy Crystal plays Mitch, a radio advertising salesperson from New York. On his thirty-ninth birthday, his station manager puts Mitch on probation for letting one of his advertisers run an obnoxious spot that hurts the "sound" of the station.

Later that day, he speaks to his son's class about what he does for a living. Danny introduces his father as a submarine commander.

Mitch has to explain to the class that he actually works at a radio station. He's not an announcer. He sells the air time that the commercials go in. The glassy-eyed children let out a collective moan. Then comes Mitch's soliloquy that begins, "Value this time in your life, kids, because this is the time in your life when you still have your choices, and it goes by so quickly. . . ."

Mitch is the true Accidental Salesperson in the throes of a midlife crisis. That evening, he questions what he's doing.

"I sell air," he complains to his wife, Barbara. He recalls his uncle, an upholsterer who, at the end of his day, had something tangible to show for the work he had done.

Mitch's buddies, Ed and Phil, are having their own midlife crises. For Mitch's birthday, they give him a trip to Colorado to participate in a cattle drive. The trail boss is Curly (Jack Palance's character), who takes one look at Mitch and sees that he's lost and unhappy. Curly explains that two weeks on the trail isn't going to cure him. Instead, Curly suggests that Mitch has to discover the "one thing," which he must figure out for himself.

Shortly after that, Curly dies. The City Slickers commit to drive the herd to the next ranch themselves. There is a huge storm. Norman, the baby bull Mitch helped deliver, is washed into a raging river. Mitch risks his life to lasso Norman and pull him to safety. The City Slickers heroically drive the herd to the next ranch only to discover that the company that stages the cattle drive is going out of business and selling the cattle they just saved to a meat processor.

The last scene shows Mitch returning to New York. His wife picks him up outside the baggage claim area at La Guardia airport.

"So, how are you?" she asks.

"Good. Things are good. Look what I found," Mitch says, pointing to his smile.

"Hmmm. That's nice. Where was it?"

"Colorado! I mean, it's always the last place you look."

"Mitch," Barbara says, "I've been thinkin'. If you really hate your job, why don't you get outta there. We'll be all right."

"No. I'm not gonna quit my job. I'm just gonna do it better. I'm gonna do everything better."

"Everything?" They kiss.

Mitch had made The Choice.

Mitch finally realized that your choices don't end when you're a little kid. Every day you are faced with a choice. You can quit your job and go do something else—or you can choose to do the job you have better.

Developing an obsession with doing it better is vital to success. In *City Slickers II,* Mitch is the general manager of the station.[4]

Until you choose to do it better, no book, tape, seminar,

or personal growth guru can help you—no matter what your career.

Getting into sales accidentally makes it hard to sell on purpose. Therefore, a crucial but simplistic step is to make some purposeful commitments:

- Make a commitment to yourself to succeed.
- Make a commitment to the company you represent.
- Make a commitment to your product or service.
- Make a commitment to your customers.
- Make a commitment to "do it better."

An axiom is a self-evident truth. It requires no proof because it is so obvious. If you buy this first axiom, you're on your way to a fulfilling and rewarding sales career.

A corollary is something that naturally flows from the axiom and therefore incidentally or naturally accompanies or parallels it. Imagine that the corollary starts with the phrase, "It follows that . . ."

Accidental Salesperson Axiom:
Your clients get better when YOU get better.

Corollary:
Your clients are praying for you to get better.
They want to work at the highest levels
with the best salespeople in the business.

Okay, you've made The Choice. You're ready to embark on your own personal sales boom. Let's get something straight. If you are going to rise to the top of any profession, you are going to have to pay some kind of price. Can you imagine putting in four years of college, four years of medical school, and then four years of residency at a hospital where you're on duty for twenty-four hours at a time, just to become a physician?

It's called delayed gratification.

Delayed gratification means sacrificing now in anticipation of a bigger reward at some future date. Not only do doctors put in twelve years of intense study and work, they take out massive loans to pay for the privilege.

You got into sales for free. But somewhere along the way you're going to have to pay the price—including study, hard work, and long hours. Today's headlines scream about the $5 million signing bonus for the quarterback or the $30 million Nike endorsement deal for a young Tiger Woods. What you **don't** see is all the work they did for free before they got paid for it.

If you're going to make an exorbitant amount of money in sales, you have to be willing to put in an enormous amount of time and energy (for free) before you are in a position to earn that money.

Sales is hard work but the rewards for many top salespeople are well worth it. Before you commit to the hard work, you must answer a very important question:

Do you need to be **wanted** or do you **want** to be **needed**?

Part of the price you pay in selling is dealing with rejection. When you sell on purpose you will start to recognize that most of what you used to call rejection is merely indifference. Still, it is easier to sell things people want to buy than it is to sell things people need but don't necessarily want to buy.

As an outside salesperson, you do a lot more work than a retail clerk. A customer who walks into a clothing store looking for a blue, double-breasted suit is already predisposed to buy. Sure, the salesperson can mess up the sale by not knowing the product, not having the product, or not being attentive. But contrast this to a scenario in which the salesperson in the blue, double-breasted suit is calling on a buyer and trying to discover a need for a new product or process. This salesperson has to sell the first meeting, sell the second meeting, and sell the client on investing enough time to determine if there is a need. Then the salesperson must persuade the prospect there is a need and develop a sense of urgency so the prospect acts. The salesperson does this by creating a vision of a more efficient and profitable operation and offering evidence that purchasing the product will result in the vision.

There is one opportunity after another to fail. Clients reject your approaches and hide from your phone calls.

That's why outside salespeople earn more money than retail clerks.

Then there are your well-meaning parents, friends, and spouse. They question how you can take the rejection and uncertainty of selling. One of my friends once told me he didn't understand how I could go to work not knowing how much money I was going to bring home at the end of the month. "That's a lot of pressure," he said.

I thought to myself, "I'd rather not know how much I'm going to make this month than be sure about how little I'm going to make. I'd rather have a job where I can get rewarded for productivity and not just get a cost of living adjustment at the end of the year."

Working on commission or some kind of salary bonus arrangement gives you the tremendous opportunity to give yourself a monthly merit increase. That's the good news.

Your clients want you to get better, but they are not always encouraging. You may get all excited about "doing it better" one day and be looking at the want ads at lunch because a client rejected you. It's going to take some time.

If you want to be needed, you will persist despite the resistance. You will make your client's lives better and businesses more profitable. Then something wonderful happens: Your clients give you referrals and your prospects promptly return your calls.

At that point, you are wanted because clients realize how much they need your expertise. You have become a partner instead of a vendor.

Sales is a series of defeats punctuated by profitable victories. If you focus on the defeats instead of the victories, you can easily lose sight of your goals. If you understand that you're paying your dues and that it does get better, you will hang in long enough to enjoy better relationships.

Accidental Salespeople don't have a philosophy of sales. Why should they? They are still deciding if they like sales. They doubt selling and themselves. It's hard to develop a philosophy "on the fly." All of a sudden you're in sales. You patch together a sales style based on salespeople you've met and as an opposite reaction to stereotypical salespeople you've seen in movies and on television.

A philosophy is a theory underlying or regarding a sphere of activity or thought. Let's start working on your philosophy of selling right now. First, let me share with you my philosophy of selling. Over the last twenty-five years I've come to firmly believe that . . .

> Life is one big seminar and lifelong learners get more out of life.

One day a brochure crossed my desk. The headline caught my eye. It read, "How to Write Brochures That Sell." The brochure advertised a six-hour seminar. The cost of the seminar seemed reasonable. I wanted to learn more about writing brochures that sell. So you know what I did?

You guessed it. I studied the brochure for three hours and incorporated all the ideas I found into my brochure. Hey, if you were trying to sell a seminar on how to write brochures, wouldn't you take your own advice when you produced the brochure? So why invest $129?

Now think about this. I've sold sales training for the past eighteen years. When I call on a prospect there is an interesting dynamic at work. He is getting a free sales clinic. I practice what I preach. He is taking in my presentation and also deciding if he wants his salespeople selling to their customers the way I sell to him.

There are sales trainers who teach tactics your gut tells you are wrong. Trust your gut. Unless you are selling time-share condominiums in Mazatlan or fake Rolex watches on the streets of New York City, avoid anything that feels funny or seems tricky. If you want repeat business and referrals, trust and truth will trump tactics.

Professional buyers go to seminars on how to spot salespeople who are using manipulative tactics. As a buyer there is nothing worse than sitting down with a salesperson who is mechanically mouthing a technique that feels foreign to him.

Imagine that you're in a car dealership and the salesperson looks you in the eye and says, "If you were my own mother, I would suggest that you buy this car today. It's that good a deal."

The salesperson wants you to think to yourself, "I guess this is a really good deal." What you're really thinking is, "What kind of a sucker does this guy take me for? I bet he says that to all his customers."

I wouldn't use a tactic like that on my own mother. I don't teach them either.

I learned lessons from the brochure on how to write brochures. Likewise, you can learn as much from a tough customer as you can from a professor or professional speaker. Some of the best sales seminars I've ever attended were free. In fact, they weren't even billed as seminars. They just turned out that way. They were "Accidental Seminars." They were powerful nonetheless.

In each chapter of *The Accidental Salesperson* I'll tell you a story of an ordinary salesperson giving an extraordinary clinic on how to sell or I'll tell you a story about a client who taught me how to sell.

Accidental Sales Training Seminar
The Shoeshine Guy

I am walking through Terminal 2 at O'Hare Airport lugging two heavy bags. I see the shoeshine stand directly ahead. The shoeshine man is looking for his next sale.

I'm walking and thinking about getting to my connecting gate.

Somehow he catches my eye. When he has it, he looks down at my shoes. My eyes follow his. As I pass, trying not to look him in the eye again, he says, "Sir, let me shine those Cole-Haan loafers for you."

"Uh, no thanks, I've got to catch a plane," I reply. (Now there's an original objection he's never heard before.)

I keep walking, but now I'm thinking, *How did he know that these are Cole-Haan shoes? That was an interesting approach. I wonder if they are Cole-Haan shoes?*

I duck into the nearest men's room and, balancing on my left foot, I take off my right shoe to read the label. It reads "Cole-Haan," and I put it back on and return to the shoeshine stand.

"I've changed my mind. I need a shine after all."

Are you willing to learn from someone who is not a trainer or teacher? This shoeshine professional sold me a $5 shoeshine and threw in seven sales success principles absolutely free. Sure, his service isn't very complex and his sales process isn't nearly as complicated as yours. At the same time, you can benefit from and form a philosophy around these seven ideas:

1. *A strong opening is critical.* When you pass the "typical" shoeshine man, he says, "Shine 'em up?" My pro had taken his approach to a higher level with a customized opening line for each customer. Research by Dartnell ranks approach/involvement the number one must-have selling skill. The same survey ranks closing at number six.[5] This shoeshine man's opening question and confirmation question are one and the same. Strong opening leads to strong closing.

2. *Product involvement is a powerful success trait.* By calling out the brand of shoe, he was communicating, "Hey, this is what I do. I care about shoes." Wouldn't you rather buy anything from a salesperson who is into what he's doing?

3. *Controlling the focus of the meeting is critical.* When I passed the shoeshine stand, I was focused on getting to my gate. The salesperson broke my preoccupation with catching a plane and forced me to focus on my shoes. When you control the focus, you gain more control of the situation.

4. *Eye contact is an important trust-building tool.* You convey confidence with eye contact. Looking customers in the

eye and smiling with your eyes and mouth both help to build trust and reduce reluctance to do business with you.

5. *Helping customers discover needs is part of the process.* By getting me to look at my own shoes, I discovered that it had been a while between shoeshines. People rarely resist their own data and discoveries.

6. *Doing it differently is refreshing and memorable for the customer.* I have passed thousands of shoeshine stands and had hundreds of shoeshines. I still remember the shoeshine guy who did it a little differently. Will your customers remember you?

7. *Customers buy from salespeople who align their behavior with the things customers value.* Customers **want** to buy things. They want to work with professionals. They want to be engaged and challenged.

Because I believe life is one big seminar, and lifelong learners get more out of life, I can get a $129 seminar out of a 50 cent brochure and I can get seven key selling strategies from a $5 shoeshine (plus tip).

Ralph Waldo Emerson said, "Life is a succession of lessons, which must be lived to be understood."

What lessons will you learn today? Who will your teachers be? You never know. Just be open to learning from everyone.

I am not a motivational speaker. Salespeople leave my seminars with a clear understanding of specific steps they can take to succeed. This "job clarity" can be very motivating.

This book will not motivate you to become successful; it will help you be more successful so that you will become motivated.

Achievement is motivating. Closing a sale can boost your enthusiasm.

Look around at the successful people you know who can afford to retire. Few of them do. They are looking for the next challenge and the next achievement.

Life is too short to demand anything less than the best

from yourself and to give anything less than your best to your customers. And being the best is a choice you can make today. Choose and you set yourself apart. You'll approach your job and your customers with a renewed sense of interest and purpose. You'll set in motion a chain of events that changes everything for the better. You can do it. You can align yourself with things that buyers value.

It's no accident that you picked up this book. It was a choice. Every day, you make choices about exactly the kind of salesperson you're going to be. Doing this consciously will set you apart from your competitors. In order to make these choices consciously, you'll need . . .

Notes

1. *Moscow on the Hudson.* 1984. Directed by Paul Mazursky. 117 minutes. Columbia Pictures Corporation, Delphi Premier Productions.
2. James P. Morgan. "Are Your Suppliers' Sales Reps Ready to Go to Bat for You?" *Purchasing,* June 3, 1993.
3. *City Slickers.* 1991. Directed by Ron Underwood. 117 minutes. Columbia Pictures Corporation, Delphi Premier Productions. Videocassette.
4. *City Slickers II.* 1994. Directed by Paul Weiland. 115 minutes. Columbia Pictures Corporation, Face Productions. Videocassette.
5. Christian P. Heide. *Dartnell's 29th Sales Force Compensation Survey 1996–1997* (Chicago: The Dartnell Corporation, 1996).

Chapter 2

The Chart

"Ladies and gentlemen, we've got to take it to the
next level."

In well-produced sales meetings at lavish resorts, CEOs and
sales managers urge their teams to "take it to the next level."

There is one major problem with these exhortations.
Most of us translate the phrase, "We've got to take it to the
next level" into "I've got to work even harder and sell even
more than I did last year." Hey, you're already working
harder, smarter, and longer than you ever imagined you
would. So hearing that you have to take it to the next level is
not very motivating, is it?

"Taking it to the next level" is just a bad business cliché
unless you have a clear picture of precisely what level you've
already attained and are able to envision exactly what the
next level will look like when you get there.

That's what we're going to do in this chapter.

When you choose to operate at a higher level, you leverage every prospect contact. It is possible to increase your sales
dramatically. It requires no more effort than you're exerting
now. Just a different kind of effort. The same territory and the
same number of presentations you made last week can yield
huge sales increases if you consciously change your selling
style.

The far-left column of Figure 2-1 describes various attri-
butes of the selling process. The row across the top names
the levels of professionalism you've achieved if you exhibit
the behaviors in the columns immediately below "Level 1,"

Figure 2-1.   The Chart helps you know exactly what level you've reached and allows you to envision exactly what the next level looks like when you get there. Notice that you can be at different levels with different clients on the same day.

	Level 1 Account Executive	Level 2 Salesperson or Problem Solver	Level 3 Professional Salesperson	Level 4 Sales and Marketing Professional
Level of trust	Neutral or distrustful	Some credibility	Credible to highly credible; based on salespersons' history	Complete trust based on established relationships and past performance
Goal/call objective	To open doors; to "see what's going on"	To persuade and make a sale or to advance the prospect through the process	Customer creation and retention; to "find the fit"; to upgrade the client and gain more information	To continue upgrading and increase share of business
Approach and involvement	Minimal or nonexistent	Well-planned; work to get prospect to buy into the process	True source of industry information and "business intelligence"	Less formal and more comfortable because of trust and history
Concern or self-esteem issue	Being liked	Being of service, solving a problem	Being a resource	Being an "outside insider"
Precall preparation	Memorize a canned pitch or "wing it"	Set call objectives; prescript questions; articulate purpose–process–payoff	Research trade magazines, Internet; analyze client's competition	Thorough preparation, sometimes with proprietary information unavailable to other reps
Presentation	Product literature, spec sheets, rate sheets	Product solution for problem they uncover during needs analysis	Systems solutions	Return on investment proof and profit improvement strategies
Point of contact	Buyer or purchasing agent	End users as well as buyer or purchasing agent	Buyers, end users, and an "internal coach" or advocate within client's company	"Networked" through the company; may be doing business in multiple divisions

DEFAULT   ▲   **PREFERENCE SETTINGS**

"Level 2," and so on. For example, you fax a product brochure to a prospect. That's Level 1: Your "presentation" consists of "Product literature, spec sheets, rate sheets." On the other hand, if you clip an article on golf course maintenance and fax it to a customer who sells turf pesticide products, your "Approach and involvement" is to be a "True source of industry information and 'business intelligence.'" With that customer, with that action, you are at Level 3.

The Chart adds a component to sales and sales training long missing: The quality component. Immediately, you can begin to apply quality standards and not just quantity standards to your sales process.

As you study The Chart, think about specific customers and prospects. Right away, you'll be able to see what level you have attained with that specific person and envision exactly what the next level is going to look like when you get there.

The Chart shows you how to work smarter.

In a *New York Times* Theater Review, Walter Goodman writes, "Whether the attention comes from academics or journalists or a playwright or two, the salesman is most commonly a figure of mockery, particularly if he is a traveling man. . . . The calling is seldom held up as an exemplar of high aspirations or edifying values."

The messages media put into our brain about selling conspire to defeat Accidental Salespeople before they even begin to discover what selling on purpose is all about.

As an Accidental Salesperson you have to confront and vanquish the stigma of selling. The Chart helps you do that. Since Arthur Miller penned *Death of a Salesman,* most media portrayals of salespeople have been negative. Miller's character Willy Loman was deeply flawed. The salespeople in David Mamet's *Glengarry Glen Ross* used high-pressure tactics and wallowed in low self-esteem. Even Pee Wee Herman ran shrieking through his Playhouse when the door-to-door salesman came calling.

You didn't get into sales to frighten people. In fact, most Accidental Salespeople chose their selling style in order not to be perceived as a typical salesperson.

Early sales training was essentially a boot camp for professional stalkers. A stalker is a person who persists despite
the wishes of another. Many states now have laws on the
books—or at least in the making—to prevent stalking.

In the early days, sales techniques and sales pressure
took precedence over solving a prospect's problem. Sales as
it's portrayed in the media and as it was taught a few decades
ago is a stressful way to make a living. I recall listening to
an early sales training record. J. Douglas Edwards was the
speaker. He was in what sounded like a packed auditorium. I
visualized him pacing the platform as he exhorted the salespeople in the audience.

"Gentlemen," he said, "when you ask a closing question,
shut up. Shut . . . up! Because the next person who
talks _____."

". . . Loses." That piece of advice by J. Douglas Edwards
has been passed down through several generations of salespeople. "The first person who talks loses" line is on the lips of
even the newest salespeople.

Think about the implications of that mindset. If you believe you are selling something that only losers buy, you will
take a hit to your self-esteem even when you make a sale.
While the Silence Close is legitimate, the idea that someone
has to lose in order to do business with us is flawed.

As Strother Martin told Paul Newman's character Cool
Hand Luke, "You've got to get your mind right."

To get your mind right, you have to have a different picture of what "good" looks like in selling. It is vital to replace the
stereotypical salesperson who stigmatizes the profession with a
vision of yourself operating at Level 2 or higher on The Chart.

In computer-speak, the option the system or software
chooses when you don't indicate a choice yourself is called
the default mode. If you don't tell your Microsoft Word software your font and type size "preferences," Bill Gates has already set the "default" at 12-point Times New Roman.

Too often, Accidental Salespeople choose a selling style
as a reaction to the negative stereotypes. If being pushy is
bad, then being more passive must be better. Accidental
Salespeople often default to Level 1. Many salespeople never

grasp that, in sales, the opposite of pushy isn't passive, but professionally persistent.

The Chart helps you make The Choice of what kind of salesperson you're going to be. Level 1 is the default mode. It's where many people who ended up in sales end up.

"I was in the neighborhood and thought I'd pop in to see if you needed anything" is a Level 1 approach.

Building a packet of product literature to take to the first meeting with the client is a Level 1 behavior.

"Anything coming down for me this week?" is a Level 1 question.

Faxing over price lists and product literature is a Level 1 activity.

As you look at The Chart, you may see that you have some clients with whom you are operating at Level 1. You may be operating at Level 2 or higher with other clients. You take your career to the next level by taking your relationship with **each client** to the next level.

Obviously, reacting to client requests is sometimes necessary. Just know that when you're doing it, you're at Level 1. Some clients may even demand Level 1 behavior because they don't know any better. It is your job to override their default mode and begin setting your own preferences.

Making a conscious choice to operate at Level 2 or higher is how an Accidental Salesperson starts to sell on purpose.

Think of Level 2 as the "base camp" from which to launch your assault on the summit of sales professionalism. Mountain climbers establish base camp part way up the mountain. They don't start their climb from the valley.

Look at The Chart to see how trust evolves. Level 4 salespeople have complete trust based on established relationships and past performance. That may take ten years. You cannot wait ten years.

Fortunately, you can get to Level 2 very early in your career. Set your preference at Level 2 and your clients will perceive you as 100 percent better than every Level 1 salesperson who approaches them—and most salespeople **are** Level 1 salespeople. Next, choose to have several Level 3 or 4 "moments" with your prospects and clients.

Have you ever clipped and sent an article about an issue or trend in the prospect's industry to that prospect? If you have, you had a Level 3 "moment." You chose to be a source of industry information and business intelligence. (You weren't necessarily at Level 3 all day though.)

You can also put Level 3 and 4 "pages" in your presentations. More on that later.

These Level 3 moments add up. They have a profound effect on your prospects and customers. Buyers may not have The Chart on their desks to rate salespeople. However, after seeing a parade of salespeople march through their offices, buyers develop a built-in rating system they apply to each salesperson.

Moving from Level 1 to Level 2 on The Chart means that you are aligning your sales behavior with those things that buyers value most in salespeople. That will make you a tough act for a competitor to follow. Prospects and clients are like Olympic figure skating judges. They rate salespeople who call on them—and there aren't many perfect scores. Here is part of a letter from a client to a sales manager who had enrolled a salesperson in one of our programs:

> Dear Kelly,
>   I am writing to tell you about the kind of service that I am getting from your sales associate, Kim Delwiche. Kim has taken our account, educated us about your services, and offered us solid information and evidence to back up her suggestions. If you don't have a nickname for Kim, may I suggest "The Yardstick"? Why "The Yardstick"? She sets the standard by which we measure all of the other salespeople in the marketplace.
>
>   Sincerely,
>   Ray Lassee, Manager

Following Kim into Ray's office would be like having to do your figure skating after Olympic gold medalist Tara Lipinski had just completed hers. No matter how good you are, you are going to be held to a higher standard by the judges.

Now here's the rest of the story. Kim had only been in her sales position for six months. She distanced herself from the pack without tricks or manipulation. She simply aligned her behavior with the behavior that prospects and clients value.

You may not have a worldwide audience like Tara Lipinski. Your clients don't pass out gold, silver, and bronze medals. They do, however, evaluate your performance daily and award the better performances with orders.

Do you think that Ray Lassee buys more from Kim than he does from the other representatives who call on him? One of the reasons is that he spends more time with her. You buy time when you gain trust.

Einstein said, "There is nothing more practical than a good theory." What I would have given to have a model like "The Chart" to plug into when I started my career in sales.

Getting a letter like Kelly's letter on Kim is one way to know that you're on track. Sometimes the feedback doesn't come in the form of a letter. It comes by the way the client reacts. Life is one big seminar. Lifelong learners get more out of life. Your clients can teach you a lot about selling by the way they react to you. Here's what one client taught me.

In 1976, I was selling radio advertising in Madison, Wisconsin. I had hair. I had a positive mental attitude. I carried a Fiberglas briefcase, wore a leisure suit, and drove an orange AMC Gremlin.

Accidental Sales Training Seminar
The Car Dealer Who Canceled His Order

In 1976 there were no car phones, no pagers, no fax machines. We had a message nail. When you walked into the office, the first thing you did was retrieve all the little pink message slips from the message nail and go through them to see which calls needed to be returned. One afternoon there was a message for me from the new manager at one of my car dealer clients. The fact that the message was on a pink slip was ironic because, in essence, the new guy was firing me.

The message read, "Bob Voss, Schappe-Conway Dodge, called. Cancel all of our advertising schedules immediately. You will have a twenty-minute meeting to re-pitch the entire year's advertising budget on Thursday. Your appointment with Mr. Voss is at 1:20 P.M."

Twenty minutes to present an entire year's advertising program. The meeting was in forty-eight hours.

The bad news: The client had canceled his advertising. The worse news: I was his 1:20 meeting. That meant he was meeting with sales reps from every media for twenty minutes each. He had an 8:00, 8:20, 8:40, 9:00, 9:20, 9:40, and so on. I was going to be the fourteenth media rep he would see that day.

Mr. Voss canceled his advertising on Tuesday. The twenty-minute meeting was set for Thursday. In preparing for the meeting, I called a salesperson at the dealership. I learned from her that Mr. Voss had just been hired away from Dodge City in Milwaukee to turn around the Dodge dealership in Madison. For those of you who can remember back that far, that was pre-Lee Iacocca, and Dodge was struggling nationwide.

I planned my approach.

I decided I didn't want to be like every other rep, in there for twenty minutes desperately presenting the year's budget. My goal was to sell Mr. Voss on the fact that twenty minutes wasn't long enough to plan a year's worth of advertising. My strategy was to differentiate myself and my presentation from that parade of media reps I imagined he was meeting with and the presentations they were making.

I made a conscious decision to not even present him a year's schedule, even though that was what he requested. I left the Arbitron local ratings book at the station. I didn't pack a rate sheet or a brochure on the station. All I had in my Fiberglas briefcase when I walked in the door was my customer needs analysis form and a notepad.

At precisely 1:20 P.M. on Thursday, the door of Mr. Voss's office opened and out came the salesperson with the one o'clock meeting. He was rolling his eyes and surreptitiously shaking his head in disgust. As he made his exit, I made my entrance. As I walked into Mr. Voss's office with my briefcase in my left hand, I extended my right hand and said, "Good afternoon, Mr. Voss, I'm Chris L– . . ."

And he said, as gruffly as you can imagine, "You're my 1:20 appointment. Sit down and pitch me." He said it in an obnoxious, but not abusive way.

"This is going to be an interesting meeting," I thought to myself. I had never been to a seminar on neurolinguistics to learn about mirroring a client, but I was astute enough to realize that here was a tough customer and I had better change my style of selling and become the salesperson he wanted me to be. Gruff, quick, and to the point. Get to the bottom line.

"Mr. Voss, I don't know if you should be on our station or not," I said. I knew he hadn't heard that line from any one of the thirteen eager salespeople who had come before me.

"What do you mean you don't know if I should be on your station or not?" he shot back.

"Well, Mr. Voss, I know that you're already a successful car dealer, and I've heard about your work with Dodge City. We're having the biggest month in the history of our radio station. So we're both successful and we're doing it without each other."

(Even when I was twenty-six years old, I wanted to see myself as providing a valuable service instead of taking someone's money.)

I looked him in the eye and said, "I work with Len Mattioli at American TV, Jon Lancaster at his dealership, and the Copps account. I'm helping them get some big sales increases.

"This is the way I work with them. See if it makes sense to you.

"Most of my important clients want ideas that help them improve traffic, sales, and profits. In order to be in a position to bring ideas instead of just rates and ratings,

I use a tool that helps me learn about nine key areas of your business that may give you an advertisable differ-ence over your competitors. It takes anywhere from an hour to an hour and one half to do this right.

"I could present a schedule and show you what your predecessor and I were working on. But I imagine you have bigger goals and tougher targets than Steve did or you wouldn't be in that chair.

"Mr. Voss, I want to be in a position to make an intelligent proposal based on your objectives and not just my need to sell you a schedule. Does that make sense?"

"Yes," he said, his voice softening a little bit.

And then I made "The Gesture." I raised my hand and gestured to his credenza and he looked around. On the credenza was a pile composed of the media kits every other salesperson had brought to the meeting.

"Mr. Voss," I said, still gesturing at the stack, "have you had any intelligent proposals so far today?"

The man changed before my very eyes. The gruff, powerful executive was now slumping in his chair. His face sagged. He looked at me and said these words: "Chris, this has been the most boring day of my life."

"Mr. Voss? Can we go through this analysis to-gether?"

"Chris, please, call me Bob."

"Bob, what are your plans for turning this dealer-ship around?"

Ninety minutes later, Bob Voss accompanied me out of his office. There were four salespeople in the wait-ing room, like planes circling over O'Hare Airport on a stormy night.

Two weeks later, the client was back on our station in a big way. They were one of the top ten advertisers on the station that year.

The most boring day of Bob Voss's life was made up of thir-teen consecutive Level 1 presentations. Level 1 selling bores clients, even if that's what they ask for. Because I approached him at Level 2, every other salesperson became an easy act to follow.

I might have made a quicker sale if I had pitched him in the allotted twenty minutes, but I don't think I would have made a bigger or longer-lasting sale. I would have been just one of the vendors he bought from, not one of the people he looked to for advertising advice and ideas.

And it doesn't matter what you're selling.

I got six lessons from that Accidental Seminar. Here they are:

1. *Tough customers don't want to deal with pushover sales-people.* By being as tough as Bob (in a polite way), I was able to win his respect. And I also didn't take it personally. "Sit down and pitch me, you're my 1:20 appointment." You know what? He probably said that to all of the salespeople who showed up at 8:00, 8:20, and so on. The only difference was that I didn't pitch him on the station. I pitched him on giving me more time. I pitched him on the way I sold instead of what I was trying to sell.

2. *You've got to be different.* Doing it differently doesn't always mean doing it better. But too many salespeople walk in to see what's going to happen and not to make something happen. The result is a bored client. It still amazes me that someone could meet with thirteen advertising reps and call it the most boring day of his life. Having an interesting approach or a different approach is vital. But you'll never get that without . . .

3. *Precall planning is vital. Dartnell's 29th Sales Force Compensation Survey 1996–1997* calls precall planning the number two selling skill (right after approach/involvement).[1] I can only tell you this. If I hadn't preplanned the call and thought about exactly what I wanted to get out of it, I wouldn't have been able to pull it off. But because I had a plan and clear objectives, I didn't get sucked into the vortex of having to pitch an annual contract in twenty minutes. I was clear about what I wanted from the call and able to get it.

4. *The customer is always right unless the customer is wrong.* But you can't come right out and tell him he's wrong. Bob Voss was buying advertising the way some of his customers were buying cars. "Give me your best deal. There are lots of competitors. If you don't have what I need, I'm going to go elsewhere," blah-blah-blah. But by taking some time to establish my own credibility and power, I was able to sell him on a better way to buy advertising.

5. *You've got to be willing to walk away from a bad deal or a bad character.* "We're having the biggest month in our station's history, and you're already a success, and we're doing it without each other." I wanted his business, but I didn't **need** his business. Approaching the client as an equal and not as a subordinate is a very difficult thing to do for young sellers and people with low self-esteem. You've got to take a tremendous amount of belief into every call—the belief that you can deliver a product or service that is of more value than the money the client is investing with you.

6. *Have friends inside the organization.* I always made it a practice to talk to the car salespeople and the office staff and the service guys so when the new manager came I could learn a little bit about him before I went to see him for the first time.

The behavior I described in the Bob Voss story resulted in a large, long-term piece of business. But if I had needed to be wanted, I wouldn't have talked to the prospect the way I did. I wanted to be needed—and that made all the difference.

Accidental Salesperson Axiom:
You can't bore people into buying.

Corollary:
Your clients buy the way you sell
before they buy what you sell.

The sooner you sell the prospect on how you are going to work together, the faster they will buy your product. This is the simplistic but profound concept that allows you to break through barriers buyers build between you and their check-books. And it brings us to . . .

Magic Phrase
"This is the way I work. . . ."

When you utter those words, you communicate to the prospect that you have an organized, planned approach to sales and to solving the problem. Understanding that sales is a process and being able to articulate the steps in your process separates you from the pack and positions you as a professional.

If you cannot sell the client on your sales process, you're going to have a tough time selling the client your product or service. Too many salespeople try to take shortcuts. If you try to sell your product before going through the process, you're going to get a lot more objections.

Bob Voss bought the way I sold that day. Two weeks later he started buying a lot of **what** I sold. It is much **easier** for the prospect to buy the way you sell too. It doesn't cost anything but a little time. Your product, on the other hand, costs money.

The strategy is simple: Starting with your next meeting, tell your prospects how you are going to sell to them before you try to sell them your product or service. There is tremendous power in the approach. Skipping this one simple step is very common and very costly to salespeople. A client who has bought the **way** you sell will buy more of the **things** you sell.

Accidental Salesperson Axiom:
Your strategy is to reveal your strategy.

Corollary:
When the clients know what's going to happen,
they can quit defending against your tactics
and start participating in the process.

The first step is selling your prospect on the way you sell. You tell the client exactly what is going to happen and when it's going to happen. Once you say the magic phrase and articulate your strategy, the air is clear, the atmosphere set. Clients don't have to guard against your tactics, because they already know what is going to happen. If your selling process requires three meetings, you say so. You indicate that the third meeting is when you'll make your presentation and ask for an order. That frees your client from a defensive response. There are no tactics to guard against.

The minute you use this strategy you'll gain an advantage over your competitors because the buyer's defensive stance is nonexistent. It isn't that you've performed a trick to remove natural defenses when you use the strategy; a defensive attitude never develops in the first place.

You already know you should spend more of your selling time listening than talking. When you tell your customers how you work and what you intend to do, you are psychologically available to listen. When you meet with a client for the first time, you aren't looking for an opportunity to slip in a line or two about how great your product is or how bad your competitor's product performs. You no longer feel the internal pressure to hurry the process along in order to quickly get to the point where you can use a closing technique. You've already sold your client on going through the steps in your selling process with you. Just follow through and back up your words with a sound needs analysis and then present your proposal. Closing becomes the natural outcome of opening the sale properly and going through the steps in your process.

Approaching the prospect properly is the key. Opening the sale takes more finesse than closing. When the client knows how you work, there is less tension and more collaboration. You become a partner instead of a pleader.

Anne Tyler's novel *The Accidental Tourist* inspired the title of this book. The story of a travel writer who detests traveling probably resonates with an Accidental Salesperson who would rather be doing something else.

$2 Sales Training Video
The Accidental Tourist[2]

Macon Leary is a travel writer who hates to travel. He writes travel books for people just like him. He advises them on how to avoid making contact with the locals and where to find familiar American food. William Hurt plays Macon, who, jarred out of his comfort zone by the senseless murder of his son, divorces his wife and falls in love with a dog trainer when he takes his dog for an obedience class.

"Never travel to a foreign country with anything you would be devastated losing," Macon advises his readers.

Macon does everything in his power to avoid the unexpected and he delights in never leaving his comfort zone, even when he has to leave the easy chair that symbolizes his comfort zone (and ours).

Macon tries to follow the path of least resistance, but the world gets to him anyway. In the end, he is forced from his easy chair into making real choices (that word **choices** again) about how to live his life.

St. Augustine wrote, "The world is a book and those who do not travel read but one page." In *The Accidental Tourist*, Macon tries to make every country just like home so he doesn't have to experience the jarring, disorienting effects of travel. But jet lag, a foreign language, driving on the other side of the road, funny colored currency, and different foods are part of the travel experience. Those things either wake up your senses and cause you to get into a new way of seeing the world or they cause you to flee to the familiar.

That's what makes *The Accidental Tourist* a powerful lesson on selling. In order to succeed, you have to leave your comfort zone, make human contact, and risk the devastating feelings of rejection. You must learn to anticipate and embrace change instead of struggling to maintain the status quo.

Seneca said, "It is not because things are difficult that we do not dare; it is because we do not dare that they are difficult."

Getting into sales accidentally has a similar jarring effect on people. You must overcome much of your early childhood experience to succeed in selling.

"Don't speak to strangers."

"Speak when you're spoken to."

"Don't brag."

And my personal favorite, "Take care."

As I write these words, I am fast approaching my fiftieth birthday. For just about all of my forty-nine years, my mother has told me "Take care" every time we say good-bye.

"I love you. Take care."

Count how many times you've heard the words "Take care" from your parents and well-meaning friends and flight attendants.

"Bye-bye. Take care."

"Bye now. Take care."

Then count the times you've heard the words "Go for it," or "Take a risk," or "Start your own business. You can do it." Or, "You'd make a great salesperson."

What are you going to do today that is uncomfortable but necessary to your own success? You're not a kid anymore, and even in an easy chair, life can find you.

It's your choice.

You've already made The Choice to commit to the sales profession (or at least to keep reading). You have The Chart, which helps you figure out which level you've achieved and helps you envision what "the next level" looks like. It would appear that you're ready to meet . . .

Notes

1. Christian P. Heide. *Dartnell's 29th Sales Force Compensation Survey 1996–1997* (Chicago: The Dartnell Corporation, 1996).
2. *The Accidental Tourist*. 1988. Directed by Lawrence Kasdan. 121 minutes. Warner Brothers. Videocassette.

Chapter 3

The Challenge

The Challenge is to choose from The Chart the kind of salesperson you're going to be every time you interact with a prospect. The moment you do that, you cease to be an Accidental Salesperson and start to sell on purpose. Instant differentiation.

Since you are competing with Accidental Salespeople, your newfound sense of purpose sets you apart. You start to set the standard for how selling is done in your industry.

There is some debate as to whether or not sales is a profession.

The Merriam Webster Collegiate Dictionary defines profession as "a calling requiring specialized knowledge and often long and intensive academic preparation." By that standard, selling is not a profession in the same way that law or medicine is.

Professionals have to meet rigorous standards in order to ply their trade. They have to pass a test. They generally choose their line of work consciously. They make sacrifices in order to be able to pursue their chosen line of work.

Our third $2 Sales Training Video ostensibly is about firefighters. On another level it is about professionalism. Ron Howard's film *Backdraft* won an Academy Award for its pyrotechnic special effects. However, there is a scene in the film that had a far more profound effect on me than the scenes that capitalize on special effects. See what kind of effect it has on you.

$2 Sales Training Video
Backdraft[1]

At the beginning of *Backdraft,* two young brothers accompany their firefighter father on a call and end up witnessing his death. It's a tough way to get your picture on the cover of *Life* magazine. The tragedy traumatizes Brian but galvanizes big brother Bull. Flash forward twenty years. Brian McCaffrey comes home to Chicago after failing in sales. He completes his firefighter training and informs his brother Stephen "Bull" McCaffrey that he too is going to fight fires.

Bull doesn't believe Brian has what it takes. My favorite scene is Bull's boat where he has moved after being kicked out of his home. Bull manages to escalate a sibling rivalry into an all-out war on his kid brother's character.

Bull to Brian: "Am I really supposed to believe you came crawling home because you felt heart strings moan for the family biz? You were bankrupt, man. The scary thing is you probably coulda got away with it for a while. Hang back a little at the fires. Aaaaah, you know the drill. The only problem is that this job is just no place to hide. It's not like having a bad day selling log cabins. You have a bad day here—somebody dies."

The story involves a mysterious set of fires that systematically kill off key people. It is the work of a clever arsonist. Brian, it turns out, is better suited as an investigator. He joins the special investigation and ultimately discovers the villain.

I hope I'm not ruining the movie for you by giving away the plot. There's a powerful message here. It's another instance of salespeople getting a bad rap in the movies.

Bull dismisses the entire sales profession with a few lines: "In this job, there is no place to hide." In sales you can drive around aimlessly or purposefully drive golf balls at the range. You don't have to put yourself in tough situations. You can hang back a little.

"This isn't like having a bad day selling log cabins." That sentence might just as well be shortened to "This isn't like having a bad day selling." Bull's implication is that salespeople don't have to uphold the high standards of firefighters.

"If you have a bad day on this job, somebody dies."

And you thought working on commissions was tough duty.

Wake up! There is no hitting the snooze button when the fire alarm sounds. It is not a job you do when you "feel" like doing it. There are no "accidental firefighters." Firefighters fight to get into the academy. They study more and train harder than most salespeople. They see themselves as professionals.

They have specialized knowledge and spend long hours in preparation.

What if **you** had a job that required you to have one good day after another or somebody would die? And that somebody could be you. Do you think you might come to work a little more focused? Would you be a little bit more "into" what you're doing?

No Bad Days!

After watching *Backdraft*, "No bad days" became a major theme for me. "No bad days" is a very high standard. It is the standard to which we routinely hold the professionals we deal with: CPAs, dentists, surgeons. A doctor who has a bad day is slapped with a malpractice suit. Professionals in many fields are required to have one good day after another.

I challenge you to examine your professionalism using the firefighters' standards—or the standards of any other professional.

Not long ago, a book called *Emotional Contagion* revealed that 75 percent of Americans consider every third day to be a bad day.[2] If that's true of you, you will have four bad months this year. Think how much more productive you could be if "No bad days" became your battle cry.

Professionals set higher standards for themselves. It's no

accident that many firefighters live to retire after twenty or thirty years of service. Their training and constant retraining prepare them to approach each fire as a professional.

It is possible to have one good day after another in sales too. But first, you have to believe it's possible. Second, you have to understand that good days are made up of good meetings, and good meetings contain conscious Level 2, 3, and 4 "moments." Having one good day after another is the choice professionals make.

Prediction: The idea of allowing yourself a bad day eventually will become a foreign concept. Of course, this means more money for you and your family, but just as important, you'll find more fulfillment and enjoyment in your career. When you sell on purpose and align your behavior with the things that prospects value, you have one good meeting after another. That is how you build one good day after another.

Professional Speakers Are Not Supposed to Have Bad Days Either

It was an important seminar for a major group. There were just twenty people in the room. However, nearly eight hundred were "attending" via satellite in dozens of other venues.

This was real-time "distance learning." It required only that the speaker travel a great distance. Five minutes before air, I walked past the group VP who had hired me.

"Are you ready?" he asked.

I answered with a question of my own: "What are my choices?"

He smiled as if he didn't mind my smart-aleck answer.

There is something wonderful about structure. Having to start and end at a specific time helps rivet attention and creates focus.

What are your choices? One of the great things about sales is that for many hours during the day, there is no one watching you. For too many salespeople that lack of structure gives them too many choices.

Having high standards for yourself and holding yourself to them is one way to create structure.

Part of the manager's job is to create structure and systems that cause people to do the right things whether they feel like it or not. It's part of your job, too. That's what pros do. "Management is doing those things necessary to deny people who work for you the unpleasant opportunity of failing." Ferdinand F. Fournies's advice is critical for you because only people who sell on purpose will set stringent standards for themselves.

The Three Secrets of Success

"Chris, there are three secrets of success," said my dinner companion. We were finishing our dessert on a flight from Chicago to San Francisco.

I rarely talk with people on airplanes because of the inevitable question they ask, "What do you do for a living?"

"I'm a professional speaker. I don't want to talk about it," I'm always tempted to say. Once people know you're a professional speaker, they have to ask, "What do you speak about?" You can end up making two or three extra talks a week on airplanes.

My dinner companion had initiated a conversation before I had chance to put on my headset or bury my nose in a book.

I asked him what he did for a living.

"I'm retired."

Amazed that such a young-looking man could be retired, I asked what he had retired from.

"Chris, I invented a software program that helps businesses track their inventory in multiple locations. We got some venture capitalists to back the company and just went public."

Life is one big seminar. I spent the next hour and a half grilling this guy.

"How did you get venture capital? How did you get your

product into Fortune 500 companies? Who did you work with to do the IPO?"

I'm sure he got tired of talking to me. Over dessert he said, "Chris, would you like to know the secret of success?"

These are the words I wrote in my diary that night. I didn't write down the name of my teacher, but we were in First Class on United, so you can trust the source.

"The first secret of success is that you have to know what you're doing." There are a lot of people who fail simply because they don't study their industry. They don't go to seminars. They don't read. And they fail. However, knowing what you're doing isn't enough.

"The second secret of success is that you have to **know** you know what you're doing." Success is a process, and repeating successful behaviors over and over again is key. But you have to know what is working so you can repeat what's working.

"The third secret of success is that you have to be known for what you know." Other people have to know you know what you're doing. When other people know you know what you're doing, they come to you for help and advice, not just for your low price.

The challenge is to choose from The Chart the kind of salesperson you are going to be during every client interaction. And to become known for what you know—and not just about what you sell.

Accidental Salespeople do make sales, but they're not exactly sure how they did it. Because they are in a reactive mode most of the day, they don't feel that they have much control over who buys what. To them, sales is "timing" and "luck."

When you begin to sell on purpose, you immediately separate yourself from the crowd of people who are selling but who don't really want to be. You make conscious daily decisions about what you're going to do and why, in order to take people through your process.

Your clients might even catch some of your increased confidence.

But, how does the client know you're a pro?

You have made The Choice. You've accepted the challenge of choosing from The Chart the kind of salesperson you're going to be on every client interaction. You're going to sell on purpose. You have decided to have one good day after another. The next step is communicating this choice to your prospects and customers so that they can differentiate the "new you" from the "old you." At the same time, you want to separate yourself from the pack of salespeople lining the lobbies of your customers' businesses.

You have to market your professionalism to the prospect.

Professionals prepare differently. Watch *Backdraft* and see how rigorously the firefighters train. Go on vacation with my friend, Don, a fifty-eight-year-old 747 captain who is taking his recertification test and see how little skiing and how much studying he does.

You want your customers to trust you. Your personal credibility and trust are vital parts of any successful salesperson-client relationship.

You've got to market your professionalism and not just sell your product.

So many salespeople skip the step of marketing what they know to the prospect, that when they don't skip it, they have an immediate point of differentiation. Here's a story that illustrates the essence of marketing professionalism.

Accidental Sales Training Seminar
Ladies and Gentlemen, This Is Your Captain Speaking. . . .

In the early nineties, US Air (now US Airways) had five crashes in five years. Airline travel is extremely safe, with a mortality risk of about 1 in 40 million. So for one airline to have five crashes in five years is an extreme example of very bad luck, pilot error, mechanical failures, and/or coincidence.

One of US Air's crashes occurred at LaGuardia Airport in New York. According to published reports, the pilot and copilot had never flown together before. It was a stormy night. As they barrelled down the runway, the pilot thought that the copilot had done the pre-flight checks. The copilot assumed the pilot had done them. Too late they discovered that nobody had done the cockpit checks. The flaps were not set properly so the airplane could not lift off. As the East River loomed off the end of the runway, an instant decision was made to abort the takeoff. They reversed the engines and put on the brakes. The landing gear collapsed and the plane slid nose up into the East River. Two passengers died and sixty-four were injured.

The FAA investigation revealed that pilot error and not weather was the chief factor in this airline accident. In fact, the headline in *USA Today* two months later read, "Tape reveals USAir crew's mistakes."

Flash forward three weeks from the US Air crash. I was sitting on an American Airlines flight out of Chicago. I was in the First Class cabin filled with business flyers on their way to their next meeting. The flight attendants did the usual safety announcements.

Then the captain flipped on his microphone and made an announcement. I suspect that he was reading from a script written by the marketing department. If not, he had decided to create one of the greatest sales pitches his airline had ever had. He said these exact words: "Ladies and gentlemen, this is your captain speaking. We are currently number two for takeoff. I have completed all of my cockpit checks and would like the flight attendants to please be seated."

The impact of the pilot's new greeting on the frequent flyers in the cabin was immediate and dramatic. My own attention perked up and my body involuntarily relaxed. Several seatmates let out a sigh of relief and visibly relaxed. The price of the ticket was the furthest thing from their minds. Any apprehension about flying today was alleviated by the very professional approach of the captain, who told us that he had done his cockpit checks.

> The big lesson: You have to market your profession-
> alism and not just assume that your clients know you're
> a pro.

Most pilots wouldn't think of taking off without doing their preflight checks. Nor would they think to point out to a passenger that they had done it. And yet, something that American Airlines pilot took for granted had a profound impact on his passengers—the airline's customers.

So what do you do behind the scenes that, if your customers knew you had done it, they would feel more comfortable doing business with you? You can have a profound effect on your customers by telling them what you do for them when they aren't looking, just like the pilot marketed his professionalism to a cabin full of uptight frequent flyers.

Magic Phrase
"In preparing for this meeting I . . ."

Airline captains operate, for the most part, behind closed doors. Similarly, most of the work you do on behalf of your customers happens behind the scenes. Customers do not think about you as much as you think about them. They have many other problems and concerns competing for their attention.

Going the extra mile is fine. **Marketing** the fact that you've gone the extra mile is how you gain extra mileage from your efforts.

The next time you meet with a prospect or customer, open the meeting with this phrase: "In preparing for this meeting I . . ."

Then quickly list two or three things you did to prepare. You will experience a new level of attention and respect from both clients and prospects. And you'll blow away competitors whose idea of a good sales opening is, "Anything coming down for me this week?"

If you don't tell them, they'll never know. Remember the big question: What are you doing behind the scenes for your clients that, if your clients knew you were doing it, they would feel more comfortable doing business with you? Once you've answered the big question for yourself, tell your clients.

Did you hit your client's Web site to gain information about the company? Make that known.

Did you make your client's problem the subject of a thirty-minute brainstorming session with the engineering department? Don't keep that a secret.

Are you getting some extra training, taking a course, or reading a book that will make you capable of better service? Disclose it early in the meeting.

Have you read any relevant books about the client's industry lately? Summarize the key points and share them with your client.

If you learned math the old-fashioned way, your teachers always made you "show your work." They wanted you to get the right answer, sure, but they also wanted to see how you arrived at the answer.

This same principle applies in sales. Clients reward people who have worked to earn their business. Showing your work is a winning strategy. That brings us to . . .

Accidental Salesperson Axiom:
Professionals put a premium on proper preparation.

Corollary:
If you tell them what you did to prepare,
your clients will appreciate you more.

Nowadays, it's common to see television features or even full-length productions that take us "behind the scenes" and tell us how a spectacular movie was made. The director and his company show us their work. They tell us how they created the special effects that triggered awe or perhaps almost scared us out of the movie theater.

The theory is that value is added when we know what went into impressing us. This behind-the-scenes peek is a new phenomenon. Movie fans in earlier eras didn't want the "spell" broken by being shown the smoke and mirrors. They didn't want their illusions shattered. But most people are different today. If anything, modern movie buffs are more impressed when they see the techniques that create the magic.

When this book was in proposal form, I was sitting in a Northwest Airlines club room. There are carrels with telephones and a place to plug in laptop computers. I returned a couple of calls and mentioned to one person that I had gotten a positive response on *The Accidental Salesperson* book proposal. After I hung up, a woman pushed her chair back from an adjoining carrel and said, "I couldn't help but overhear the title of your book. I'm an accidental salesperson. I was a radiology nurse. Now I sell the equipment I used to use with patients."

I sent her copies of the first three chapters. She e-mailed me to say, "I always prepare extensively for meetings with present or potential customers, but I never really let them know about it beforehand. I have started using your method to start the meeting by mentioning it and have gotten immediate, positive results."

When she read the idea, it made immediate sense to her to market the effort she was making to the client.

Hard work is rewarded, but not if your customers don't know about it.

You have a choice of airline carriers. Your customers have a choice of vendors. It may seem that price is the only point of differentiation in a product or service.

However, in highly competitive businesses, **how** you sell what you sell may be more important than the product or service you sell.

How does your client know you're a pro? Tell the client what you did to prepare.

The first Magic Phrase was "This is the way I work."

The second Magic Phrase is "In preparing for this meeting, I . . ." That lets the customer know what you did when he or she wasn't looking. It helps you become known for what you know and do for the customer.

Why do so many salespeople ignore these two powerful steps in the sales process? There are at least three reasons:

1. Salespeople assume the buyer knows why they are there, so there is no reason to talk about the way they work.

2. Level 1 sales meetings and sales training sessions put the focus on the product and not on the relationship.

3. It has taken so long to get the meeting that salespeople think this is their big chance and go for it all.

In this section, you've gained the theoretical underpinnings that solidly ground you in a proven philosophy of selling. But sales philosophy will only take you so far. Now you have to apply what you've learned.

Too many books and too many sales trainers tell you what to do without telling you why to do it. You now know that aligning your sales behavior with what clients **want** will help them see you as a professional.

You understand why it is vital to sell the client on your process before skipping ahead to the product. Here's a quick way to become known for what you know. Use the template in Figure 3-1 to send or fax articles to your customers (a full-size copy is available free from our Web site).

Marketing yourself as a source of industry information and business intelligence is a Level 3 approach that will help you accelerate your sales success.

Having more conscious Level 3 moments is another way to become known for what you know. When you mail or fax a clipping on a business issue, first mount it on a sheet that brands your company and you personally as the source of this information. You can download a letter-sized copy of this form from our Web site and simply insert your company's logo in the space provided. You can use this as a "service" touch or as part of a sophisticated system for getting appointments with hard-to-see prospects. We'll detail that system in a later chapter, but you can use this tool today.

Figure 3-1. Use this template to "brand" your Level 3 seeds.

TO:		
FROM:		No. of Pages

[INSERT LOGO HERE]

```
Information about business issues and trends
I wanted to be sure you saw.
```

[REPEAT LOGO AND ADD
POSITIONING STATEMENT HERE]

[INSERT YOUR NAME AND HOW
TO REACH YOU HERE]

Notes

1. *Backdraft.* 1991. Directed by Ron Howard. 135 minutes. Trilogy Entertainment Group, Universal Pictures, Imagine Films Entertainment. Videocassette.
2. Elaine Hatfield, Richard Rapson, and John Cacioppo. *Emotional Contagion* (Paris: Cambridge University Press, 1994).

Part 2

Transforming Sales Departments into Sales Forces

Chapter 4

Sales Department or Sales *FORCE?*

"Chris, we have some highly paid salespeople who have developed extraordinary faxing skills. I wish they could develop extraordinary selling skills."

I had asked the general manager the outcome she wanted from the upcoming seminar. With these two sentences she articulated one of the critical differences between a sales department and a sales **FORCE**. In managing by walking around, she had observed more faxing than face-to-face contact.

She was very concerned.

She hadn't seen The Chart, but knew that her highest paid salespeople were reacting to requests and processing business instead of initiating new sales and taking their prospects through the sales process. She had already calculated the bottom-line savings of replacing these reactive salespeople with clerks. The going rate for people with extraordinary faxing skills is much closer to $6 an hour than the six figures she was paying some of her salespeople. She knew one way to cut the cost of sales was to cut commissions on transactional business (or business that could be done by fax).

In *The Empire Strikes Back,* Luke asks Master Yoda, "Is the dark side stronger?"

Yoda replies, "No . . . no . . . no. Quicker, easier, more seductive."

It may be a stretch to call Level 1 the dark side of selling.

But you'll have to agree that Level 1 is easier and more seductive. Accidental Salespeople are often seduced by the "busyness" of their day. When you are selling on purpose, you will put a premium on initiating business instead of merely reacting to inquiries.

It is easier to land a sales job than it is to land a major new account. Becoming a force of one in sales requires dedication, training, focus, and resolve. Prospects test your dedication daily and your resolve regularly.

Accidental Salesperson Axiom:
The most important thing you can do is propose your solution to the prospect face-to-face and ask for the order.

Corollary:
The second most important thing you can do
is get into position to do the most important thing.

United Airlines understands that it is not in the airline business. It is in the communication business. It helps bring buyers and sellers together. A few years ago, United Airlines aired a TV commercial featuring a company president who had just called a sales meeting. His company's biggest customer had just "fired" them. Seems the customer was dissatisfied with the lack of personal attention and tired of doing business by fax. The president's solution? Give everybody an airline ticket to go see the customers. He was going to go see the customer who had just fired them himself.

It's easier to fax and e-mail than get on an airplane or hop in a car and go see someone. Just don't be fooled by thinking the easier way is the better way.

Many companies have sales departments. Fewer have sales **FORCES**. There are seven critical differences between a sales department and a sales **FORCE**. To transform yourself from a member of a sales department into a "force" of one, you need to operate on the right-hand side of the chart in Figure 4-1 instead of the "dark side."

Figure 4-1. There is more risk and rejection when you decide to be a force of one. There is also opportunity for greater accomplishments and the rewards that go with them.

Members of a Sales Department	Members of a Sales Force
• Have extraordinary faxing skills	• Have extraordinary selling skills
• Take orders and get buys	• Influence decisions and persuade
• React to inquiries	• Initiate new business
• Process business	• Take prospects through their process
• Have a commodity fixation	• Have a high-margin mindset
• Meet the buyer's criteria	• Negotiate and help set the criteria
• Talk to purchasing department	• Talk to end users

It is easy for the Accidental Salesperson to become trapped on the left-hand side. Some buyers actually try to keep you in Level 1 and out of their offices by telling you, "Just fax (or e-mail) it to me."

Prospects protect their time by not meeting with every salesperson. You can understand why. They have come to expect time-wasting, product-focused presentations from the salespeople who come calling. They would rather get that information by fax than carve out an hour to meet with an Accidental Salesperson who wanders in and wings it. By asking for a fax, they figure they'll avoid one more time-consuming Level 1 meeting.

Recognize and resist this ploy.

A critical aspect of selling on purpose is understanding that the buyer is not all knowing or all powerful. Understand that you have a product or service that solves a problem and that you can bring information and expertise to the table the customer does not have.

You dial the phone and get the prospect on the line. The trap is set as soon as the prospect says, "I'm interested. Send me some literature." At this point, Accidental Salespeople move into their reactionary mode. They are delighted that the prospect has shown some sign of interest. They dutifully write down the address. They hang up and hurry over to the shelving unit that holds the product literature. They quickly pull ten or twenty pieces of paper from the piles and place them in the company folder. Then it's off to the mail room to have the kit overnighted to the hot prospect.

Two days later, our Accidental Salesperson is shocked to learn that the hot prospect hasn't read this meticulously prepared package of product literature. In fact, she's not sure where it is.

"It's around here somewhere. Tell you what, call me in a week."

This Accidental Salesperson is lured into a Level 1 interaction by the prospect, trapped into reacting to a request instead of finding a problem or need. To avoid that situation once and for all memorize . . .

Magic Phrase

"(Gasp!) We don't have an off-the-shelf promotional kit that we send out. We customize everything. What would you like in your kit?"

When a prospect asks for your company's brochure or promotional kit, use that magic phrase. The audible gasp makes it appear you're shocked by the request. Nobody wants an off-the-shelf solution anymore, so the prospect won't object to a customized information package. By asking the prospect what he would like in the kit, you find out what the prospect thinks he needs to make a decision. You discover how sophisticated this prospect is by the type of information he requests. If the prospect doesn't know what he wants, you simply ask several questions about what he is using now and how satisfied he is with it.

"What are you using now?"
"What do you like about it?"
"Any concerns?"
Do a little selling. Say, "The way I work is to send only

things that will benefit you, and I'd rather find the one piece of paper that gives you information of value instead of having you wade through hundreds of pages of product literature."

When you respond to a request for information, it is vital that you get an agreement that the prospect will read what you send and give you feedback on it. Assert yourself. Say, "I am committing to provide the information you requested and all I ask in return is that you take my next call and tell me if you are a prospect or not. At that point we decide whether or not there is a next step. "Can we work together on that basis?"

If you can't sell the prospect on that step, you have a choice to make. Politely terminate the conversation or waste your time and $10 to overnight something to someone who hasn't bought the way you sell and probably will never buy what you sell.

Once you get the prospect to agree, explain exactly what is going to happen.

"I'm going to overnight you three pieces of paper via FedEx. There will be a cover sheet to alert your mail room. It will say, 'Information you requested on May 21.' I will call you the following morning to provide more information and measure your interest level."

One of the best investments you can make is a little rubber stamp that says, "Information You Requested on _____ _____ _____." Prospects get so much junk sent to them that they may not recognize your priceless package. The stamped notice reminds them it's material they're looking for.

Transforming sales departments into sales forces is an obsession with me. Let's look at Figure 4-2 on page 56.

A sales department has many Level 1 salespeople. A sales **FORCE** has Level 2 salespeople who have conscious Level 3 and Level 4 "moments."

Clients recognize and respond to Level 2 and higher behavior. They can feel the difference.

Figure 4-2. Members of a sales department spend most of their time at Level 1. Members of a sales force choose to operate at Level 2 and have conscious Level 3 and Level 4 "moments."

	Level 1 Account Executive	Level 2 Salesperson or Problem Solver	Level 3 Professional Salesperson	Level 4 Sales and Marketing Professional
Level of trust	Neutral or distrustful	Some credi...	Credible to highly credible; based on salespersons' history	Complete trust based on ...shed relationships and past performance
Goal/call objective	To open door; to "see what going on"	To persuade and make a sale or to advance the prospect through the process	Customer creation and retention; to "find the fit"; to upgrade the client and gain more information	To continue upgrading and increase share of business
Approach and involvement	Minimal or non-existent	Well-planned; work to get prospect buy into the process	True source of industry information and "business intelligence"	Less formal and more comfortable because of trust and history
Concern or self-esteem issue	Being liked	Being of service; solving a problem	Being a resource	Being an "outside insider"
Precall preparation	Memorize canned pitch or "wing"	Set call objectives; prescript questions; articulate purpose–process–payoff	Research trade magazines, Internet; analyze client's competition	Thorough preparation, sometimes with proprietary information unavailable to other reps
Presentation	Product literature, spec sheets, rate sheets	Product solution of problem they uncover during need analysis	Systems solutions	Return on investment proof and profit improvement strategies
Point of contact	Buyer or purchasing agent	End users as well as buyer or purchasing agent	Buyers, end users, and an "internal coach" or advocate within client's company	"Networked" through the company; may be doing business in multiple divisions

DEFAULT ▲ **PREFERENCE SETTINGS**

You will be fortunate indeed if in your career you have a true Level 4 relationship with a handful of customers. Getting complete trust and gaining access to proprietary information can take many years. However, you can go to Level 2 today with every customer and prospect you meet. You do not want to spend any time (if you're a rookie) or any **more** time (if you're a veteran) at Level 1.

You never get a second chance to make a good first impression. If you've made a Level 1 impression, your prospects will appreciate the new Level 2 you (refer back to Figure 4-1). The Lytle Organization markets an industry-specific distance learning program for sales managers. In one of the assignments, the sales manager coaches a salesperson through the process of preparing and presenting a client-focused, Level 2 proposal to a real prospect. Often, this is a first for the salesperson and the prospect. Here is one sales manager's report about how she coached a salesperson through that proposal-writing process. We call it . . .

The Tommy Transformation

Tommy is a very independent person and not very detail-oriented. He agreed to do the rough outline himself. We planned to go over it in our Wednesday one-on-one meeting. Wednesday came and Tommy had not begun work on the proposal. This was a slight problem since the presentation was on Monday and Tommy was taking Friday off.

I got up, closed the door, and explained to Tommy how the kind of presentation taught in the correspondence course would positively impact his closing ratio and his wallet. We got to work on it together. We went through a rough outline of each section.

He agreed to work on it some more that evening and have lunch with me the next day to show me the final presentation. The proposal he brought to lunch on Thursday was the best I have ever seen out of him. He also seemed to be very proud of what he had done and asked if he could practice presenting it to me in the conference room. He did great! I threw some pretty tough objections at him and he had well-thought-out answers for most of them.

On Monday afternoon Tommy called from his car to ask for "good luck." About thirty-five minutes later my phone rang again. It was Tommy calling from the prospect's office with a question the prospect had raised that he couldn't answer.

Fifteen minutes later the phone rang again and it was Tommy on his car phone yelling, "We've got the deal!"

The story doesn't end there. Mr. Green (the new client) called me Tuesday morning to ask a question about his order since Tommy was out of the office. After I answered his question, Mr. Green asked me, "What did you do to Tommy?" When I asked what he meant he said, "Tommy has been trying to get my business for four months now. He has given me a lot of information and specifications about your company and service. One of the reasons I haven't done business with your company until now was because he never seemed very organized, and my rep at the other company was always very organized. I just felt like they would take better care of my money.

"Suddenly Tommy comes in here yesterday and all his ducks were in a row. He showed me he had paid attention to what I had said I wanted to do with my business, had a program all worked out, and even got the answers to my questions right then by calling you instead of saying he would get back to me. You know, I saw a whole new side of him. I really like the young man and I'm happy to finally be doing business with him and your company. Whatever you did to him, do some more of it."[1]

Mr. Green noticed Tommy's transformation from Level 1 to Level 2.

You become a "force of one" when you align your behavior with the things your customers value in a salesperson.

Marketing expert Jay Abraham advises us that "leverage" is getting better results from the same effort or expenditure. Tommy wasted four months of meetings by operating at Level 1. Think about that. After four months of Level 1 presentations, Tommy turns it around with one Level 2 presentation. There is a tremendous amount of leverage in moving up just one level. Tommy moved to Level 2 and walked away from that meeting with an order.

That's leverage.

As long as you are going to go to the time, effort, and expense of getting in front of a prospect, you might as well make the most of it. That means making sure you have a Level 2 foundation for the meeting. It may mean having some Level 3 and 4 moments too.

A Level 2 approach is 100 percent better than a Level 1 approach, but in the case of Tommy's transformation, a Level 2 approach proved **infinitely** better than his old Level 1 approach.

Research from Learning International reveals, "The top three reasons people buy have nothing to do with price and relate directly to the quality of a sales force."

According to the survey, the three things more important than price are "business expertise and image, dedication to the customer and account sensitivity and guidance."[2]

Mr. Green noticed Tommy's newfound business expertise and image by saying, "Suddenly Tommy comes in here and all his ducks were in a row."

He described Tommy's dedication to the customer in these words: "He showed me he had paid attention to what I had said I wanted to do with my business."

Tommy demonstrated account sensitivity and guidance, in Mr. Green's estimation, because "he had a program all worked out, and even got the answers to my questions right then by calling you instead of saying he would get back to me."

The survey said, "It's the quality of the salesperson—his or her knowledge and his or her ability to bring added value to the sales—that converts prospects into buyers."

"I saw a whole new side of him yesterday."

Your customers can see a whole new side of you today. Your subtle shift in behavior will make a major impact on your prospects. And your income. The fastest way to take your sales to the next level is to identify where you are with each of your prospects and customers. Then do one or two things in the next column to the right of Figure 4.2.

Based on the box office receipts of his films, one could call producer/director George Lucas a sales genius. The first Star Wars Trilogy grossed more than a billion dollars.

You can learn something about sales from watching our next sales-training video.

$2 Sales Training Video
The Empire Strikes Back[3]

A long time ago, in a galaxy far, far away, epic heroes battled larger than life villains in the Star Wars Trilogy. At the beginning of *Empire,* Darth Vader is helping the Empire crush the rebellion. The Empire attacks the new rebel outpost on the frozen planet Hoth. Hans Solo, Princess Leia, and Chewbacca escape to Bespin and Cloud City. Luke Skywalker, urged posthumously by Obe Wan Kenobi, journeys to the planet Dogbah, where he crash lands into the swamp.

Luke has gone to Dogbah to seek out Master Yoda. After emerging from his partially submerged X-Wing fighter he encounters a "creature."

Based on the creature's appearance, Luke dismisses the creature and tries to distance himself from the little Muppet so he can find Yoda. Luke tells him he is looking for someone.

"Looking?" says Yoda. "Found someone you have I would say, hmmm?"

"Right . . ."

"Help you I can. Yes, hmmmm," says the creature.

"I don't think so. I'm looking for a great warrior."

"Ohhh! Great warrior!" says Yoda, laughing. "Wars not make one great!"

Once Luke realizes that the diminutive creature is

the Jedi whom he is seeking, the training commences. Like a sales manager trying to get people to pursue big goals, Yoda pushes Luke to maximize his potential. After Luke has practiced with rocks, Yoda suggests that Luke use The Force to raise his X-Wing fighter from the swamp. Only the tip of its nose shows in the lake.

"Oh, no. We'll never get it out now."

"So certain are you. Always with you it cannot be done. Hear you nothing that I say?"

"Master," says Luke, "moving stones around is one thing. This is totally different."

"No! No different! Only different in your mind. You must unlearn what you have learned."

"All right, I'll give it a try," Luke says begrudgingly.

"No! Try not. Do. Or do not. There is no try," insists Yoda.

Luke closes his eyes and concentrates on the task. The X-Wing slowly begins to rise from the lake. Luke cannot keep his concentration and the fighter splashes back into the lake.

"I can't. It's too big."

"Size matters not. Look at me. Judge me by my size, do you? Hm? Mmmm."

Yoda explains to Luke that The Force is in every-thing—the rocks and even the ship. It is an ally.

"You want the impossible," says Luke.

Quietly Yoda turns toward the X-Wing fighter. With his eyes closed and his head bowed, he raises his arm and points at the ship. Soon, the fighter rises above the water and moves forward as R2 beeps in terror and scoots away. The entire X-Wing moves majestically, surely, toward the shore. Yoda stands on a tree root and guides the fighter carefully down toward the beach.

Luke stares in astonishment as the fighter settles down onto the shore. He walks toward Yoda and says, "I don't . . . I don't believe it."

"That is why you fail."

During his Jedi training session, Luke finds out that Han and Leia are in danger in Cloud City. Yoda pleads with him, "Luke! You must complete your training." Despite that, Luke leaves his training early to rescue his friends. He confronts Darth Vader. The ensuing battle sets up the *Return of the Jedi* sequel. (Another great sales ploy.)

Yoda is like many demanding sales managers who try to get their people to think bigger thoughts and dare to do greater things. There are three lessons you can take from Luke Skywalker's training that will put your sales into hyperspace.

1. *Your best teachers may not look like teachers.* Luke was unwilling to accept that Yoda could teach him anything because of the way he looked. (Remember the shoeshine guy at O'Hare?) Most of the best training you get won't come from people who look like trainers.

2. *Wars do not make you great.* The key to success in sales is not to overcome objections, but to prevent them. Not having to fight is better than fighting.

3. *Your beliefs are important.* Luke didn't believe he could raise the ship, and so he couldn't. Belief in your product, your company, and yourself plays a tremendous role in sales success.

Becoming a force of one in sales requires dedication, training, focus, and resolve. Prospects test your dedication and resolve every day.

Accidental Salespeople with talent but no training can quickly lose resolve and take the easy way.

Yoda's last words to Luke as he went off to fight Darth Vader were, "Mind what you have learned. Save you it can."

Throughout the Star Wars Trilogy, people in the know say to their friends, "May The Force be with you."

I have a different wish for you. Here it is. To the company you represent and to the clients you serve, "May you be The **FORCE**."

You know the way. Just follow your "Chart."

Notes

1. Suzanne Reynolds. Assignment for "Manager for Radio Marketing" course. (May 9, 1994).
2. Jon Conlin. "Training in Turbulent Times," *Sales and Marketing Management,* July 1993.
3. *The Empire Strikes Back.* 1980. A George Lucas film directed by Irvin Kershner. 127 minutes. Lucas Film, Limited. Videocassette.

Chapter 5

Lessons from "The Tour"

Developing a High-Margin Mindset

"I'm not going to quit my job. I'm just going to do it better," said Mitch, Billy Crystal's character in *City Slickers*. Speaking of Crystal, Waterford has been "doing it better" when it comes to making and selling fine crystal for more than two hundred years.

Sarah McCann is my partner and wife. One day she announced that she had booked three seminars in Ireland. What she didn't tell me was that she also had a tour of the Waterford Crystal factory on our itinerary.

"We're traveling through Waterford today. I'd like to go take the factory tour. How about it?" Sarah said.

"Don't we have enough crystal?"

"Are you kidding? We always need more crystal. Besides, we'll never be able to buy Waterford Crystal cheaper than we can at the factory."

Remember those words, because the Waterford Crystal factory tour turned out differently than we expected. In fact, it turned into . . .

Accidental Sales Training Seminar
The Waterford Crystal Tour

After a forty-two-mile trip on narrow Irish roads lined with hedgerows, we arrive at the Waterford Crystal factory and follow the signs to "The Tour." They are selling tickets for the next tour, which starts at 11:00 A.M. We buy two tickets for two pounds each and the very pleasant ticket seller invites us to "Please wait in our gallery."

Lesson 1. Qualify your prospects for interest and money early in the sales process.

Dazzling is the best way to describe the gallery. You cannot buy anything here. You can only marvel at the beautiful pieces. There's a magnificent chandelier and art-gallery quality crystal designed by Waterford's masters. There are replicas of professional golf trophies and the crystal football that goes to the number one NCAA Division I football team in the United States.

Lesson 2. Let your prospects know early on that you have worked with other prestigious clients. People feel more comfortable when they know other smart buyers have recognized quality.

At 11:00 A.M. we board one of three buses. More than 250,000 people take this tour each year. About 120 of us are taking it now. As we move toward the first stop, our uniformed guide tells us, in her intriguing Irish accent, that Waterford's aim is not to be the largest crystal maker in the world. Just the best.

We learn that the creation of every piece of Waterford Crystal celebrates a tradition of perfection in craftsmanship dating back to 1783. Little has changed since George and William Penrose first opened their glassmaking factory in 1783.

We enter the "blowing room." Here, huge furnaces

transform the mix of silica sand, potash, and letharge into molten crystal. Teams of blowers and apprentices stand around each furnace, where they pour 1200 degree molten liquid into molds from which they will blow wine goblets this particular day. We learn that the blowers' skills are essential to Waterford Crystal because of the depth at which the facets will be cut into the crystal at a later stage. Our guide mentions that it takes five years of apprenticeship before a glassblower can make a product that leaves the factory and goes into a customer's home.

Lesson 3. Tell stories about the founder and the vision. Don't just sell your product; sell the people who are behind the product. This humanizes your company and adds value.

The Tour proceeds to the cutting room, where cutters work to release the light trapped in the crystal by the intense heat. We see that there is a rough geometric guide of the design marked onto the blank crystal. Very rough. The cutter renders the ultimate position and depth of the cut by his own sight and feel. There are two types of cuts—wedge and flat. We watch the whirring diamond-tipped "cutting" wheels that create deep intricate cuts, the hallmark of Waterford. High-powered vacuums draw crystal dust from the air at hundreds of these cutting stations. The guide explains that it takes an encyclopedic knowledge of Waterford patterns and cuts to do this job. That's because each cutter cuts each design strictly from memory.

There are no shortcuts. No two pieces are ever exactly alike. It takes eight years of apprenticeship to become a cutter and requires great strength to keep the crystal firm against the wheel. There's more. If a cutter goes one "silly millimeter" too far with what is essentially a high-speed, diamond-edged saw, he can put a hole in a goblet or vase. Since there are no "seconds" at Waterford (we learn this in the middle of The Tour), the piece is rejected and the cutter loses part of his piecework pay. The goblet is smashed and goes back to the furnace to begin the process again.

Lesson 4. Build value into the product at every stage of your sales or manufacturing process.

The guide makes sure we see a defective piece. She also shows us the "graduation bowl." In order to pass from apprentice to cutter, you must put every cut into the bowl. You have three, twenty-hour exams to do it to the exacting Waterford standards. Fail and you cannot be a cutter. Pass and you get to keep your job and the graduation bowl. It's your diploma for eight years of apprenticeship.

Lesson 5. Market the training your people go through and the standards to which they are held, not just your product.

At the next stop, we observe engravers putting decorations into various pieces of crystal. Waterford has the largest copper-wheel engraving department in the world. Engravers have even more status than cutters and blowers, having taken twelve years to master their part of the process.

I look at my watch as we enter the shipping room. We're about forty-four minutes into The Tour. Workers add the distinctive Waterford seahorse logo to the product. Our guide lets us pick up the merchandise to find the seahorse, our assurance that it is made by the artists we saw in the factory that we just toured.

Lesson 6. Get people involved with your products. Let people in on some "insider information" that not every buyer would know to look for.

In the shipping room our tour guide explains Waterford's pricing policy. Waterford Crystal doesn't make a piece until it's ordered. So even if we buy crystal in the shop, we can't take it home today. No, the people we've just seen will make it in the factory we have just toured. They will ship it to us as it comes off the line.

Our guide also tells us that the prices in the shop are the same as they are going to be in Dublin or even Chicago. In fact, the only reason to stop to shop here is that we can see a complete set of every Waterford pattern. Few department stores or jewelry stores can display the whole line.

We board the bus one more time for the quick trip to the gift shop. We go into the gift shop fully aware that there are no "seconds" and no deals. We came to Waterford to buy crystal for less. We buy more crystal at full retail than I could have imagined. And we are not alone.

Lesson 7. When you take people through every step in your process and build value into your product, price is no longer the key issue. Educated customers buy more confidently and spend more freely.

I witness a buying frenzy as bargain hunters turn into discerning crystal connoisseurs. My fellow tour members queue at cash registers. Salesclerks scan the proffered plastic through the machines so quickly you wonder if it might melt. I marvel at the number of people who thought they were going to get a deal but who are now lining up to pay full retail price.

Lesson 8. Your own facility is a powerful visual aid. Selling prospects on taking a tour is easier than selling them product. Selling them product is easier after they've taken the tour.

I paid two pounds to take a tour of the Waterford Crystal factory. We paid a lot more than that for the wine glasses, rocks glasses, brandy snifters, cake knife, limited edition vase, and the seahorse souveniers.

But the sales training was free.

Buyers who see only price lists and catalogs have trouble differentiating your product from that of your competitors. One of the most frightening words in business today is "commoditization." When your product becomes a commodity, the customer sets the price and your company loses control of the ability to earn a profit. The strategy of sending your prime prospects and good customers airplane tickets and inviting them to tour your facility is a good one. A well-orchestrated tour can sell more than the same money pumped into color catalogues and ads in trade magazines.

Using your facility and your people as "visual aids" will help bond buyers to you and help them understand why your product is worth what you charge for it. An educated customer buys more.

It's more than getting the client on your turf. It's getting the client to see the company behind the product. Seeing where the product is made, who is making it, and how they make it puts value into the product.

Accidental Salesperson Axiom:
Selling is teaching. Teaching is selling.

Corollary:
An educated customer buys your value proposition
whereas an uneducated customer buys on price.

By taking us through every step in the manufacturing process, Waterford was able to get full price for its products. When you skip steps in your sales process and jump too quickly to the close, you'll encounter more objections and price resistance.

Have you ever skipped steps in your sales process? Have you ever had someone raise an objection that you could have headed off by going through all the steps? Wouldn't it be nice to have a predictable sales process like Waterford has?

You're about to get just that.

Shortly after The Tour, I began developing a new tool.

The "Ten Most Wanted List" gives you an easy way to put ten prospects into your sales process and track their progress. It also puts you in control of making your budget. You quit worrying about one client coming through with a big order.

Here's what I mean. There are two things I hear at most of the seminars I conduct. Someone always tells me that her situation, industry, or customer is "unique" and that none of these principles will work for her. Another person will approach me and want to play "Stump the Trainer." That's the game that always begins with this statement: "Chris, I have this one client that's driving me crazy. . . ." The player then proceeds to describe an impossible-to-sell prospect who is mentally unbalanced, abusive, or both.

The player asks, "What would you do in my situation?"

Most often my answer is, "If you had ten prospects in process, you wouldn't be worried about this one prospect. You would drop him and go see someone else."

You have two choices:

1. You can worry about that one prospect.
2. You can trust your process.

However, you can only trust your process if you understand the specific steps and calculate the ratios at each stage.

Here is a sample **Ten Most Wanted List.** You load it with ten prospects and then take them through (in this example) a 16-step process.

Please take time to read the sixteen steps on this form. Your selling cycle may be shorter or longer; chances are longer rather than shorter. (Your engineers may have to meet their engineers, etc.) The bottom line is that there is a clearly identifiable process that you take every prospect through.

This one tool puts you in control by showing you where you are with every prospect and what your next step in the process will be. It lets you measure ratios at every stage of your process. In the example in Figure 5-1, the salesperson closed 75 percent of the presentations she made, so you see a 75 percent closing ratio of sales written for presentations made. However, the salesperson started with ten prospects

Figure 5-1. Some trainers have a four-step selling system. Breaking the process down into sixteen steps helps you focus on the little things you have to do to propel the sale forward.

Ten Most Wanted List

The 16-Step Selling Process Box Score

Based on your own selling cycle, set a time frame to accomplish all 16 steps.

1. Identify businesses (prospects/clients)
2. Identify decision maker

Column headers (angled):
3. Seed (describe)
4. Seed (describe)
5. Letter
6. Dial
7. Contact decision maker
8. Book first appointment
9. Confirm the first appointment
10. Complete 1st app't; Sell your process & frame the issue
11. Book Customer Needs Analysis
12. Complete Customer Needs Analysis
13. Book the proposal
14. Write the proposal
15. Make the proposal
16. Confirm the order (close)

Prospect	3.	4.	5.	6.	7.	8.	9.	10.	11.	12.	13.	14.	15.	16.
Warner Communications / Sandy Lewin (6/10) / 608-288-3044	6/10 WSJ art.	6/14 USA Today art.	6/18	6/24	6/24									
CBM Companies / Walter Cornwallis (6/10) / 715-223-3900	6/10 WSJ art.	6/10 WSJ art.	6/18	6/24										
Design Concepts / Julian Albrecht (6/12) / 414-221-2623	6/12 G.M. mag art.	6/15 WSJ art.	6/18	6/21 6/24	6/24	6/24 for 6/28	6/24	6/28	6/28 for 7/7	7/7	7/7 for 7/18	7/10	7/18	7/18 $17,354
Royal Oaks / Vicky Mertens (6/14) / 651-748-7085	6/15 G.M. mag art.	6/19 USA Today art.	6/21	6/21 6/24 6/27	6/27	6/27 for 7/5	7/2	7/5	7/5 for 7/13	7/13	7/13 for 7/21	7/18	7/21	7/21 $45,050
Gemini Systems / Fred Atkinson (6/12) / 612-584-9683	6/12 USA Today art.	6/16 left Atlas	6/25	6/28 7/8										
WPSS / Ayssa Jones (6/13) / 412-998-1587	6/13 G.M. mag art.	6/18 WSJ art.	6/21	6/25	6/25	6/25 for 6/27	6/25	6/27						
Network King / Randy Schuelling (6/14) / 608-828-3287	6/15 G.M. mag art.	6/18 USA Today art.	6/22	6/27	6/27	6/27 for 7/6	7/1	7/6	7/6 for 7/12	7/21	7/12 for 7/19	7/13	7/19	7/19 tor $5,755
New Frontiers Computer / And Keller (6/15) / 651-388-9522	6/15 G.M. mag art.	6/18 USA Today art.	6/21	6/26 6/27	6/27	6/27 for 7/5	7/2	7/5	7/5 for 7/15	7/15	7/15 for 7/22	7/18	7/22	call in 30 days
Raymond Enterprises / Tom Raymond (6/16) / 715-723-9723	6/16 G.M. mag art.	6/19 left Atlas	6/23	6/28	6/28	6/28 for 7/1	6/28	7/1						
Ermatinger Interstate / Anne Isaacs (6/17) / 612-442-3875	6/17 USA Today art.	6/21 left Atlas	6/25	6/29	6/29	6/29 for 7/3	6/29	7/3						

Totals

Decision makers ID'd ÷ total prospects	Contacts ÷ dials	App'ts confirmed ÷ appt's booked	CNA booked ÷ 1st app't completed	Proposals booked ÷ CNAs	Proposals made ÷ prop's written	Sales closed ÷ prospects started
100	80	100	57	100	100	30
% Decision makers ID'd	% Reached	% App'ts conf'd	% CNAs booked	% Prop's booked	% Prop's made	Gross Closing Ratio

Dials ÷ decision makers ID'd	App'ts booked ÷ contacts	1st app't completed ÷ appt's confirmed	CNAs completed ÷ CNAs booked	Prop's written ÷ prop's booked	Sales closed ÷ prop's made
100	87.5	100	100	100	75
% Decision makers dialed	% App'ts booked	% App'ts completed	% CNAs completed	% Prop's written	% Closed

(and presented to four), so 30 percent of the people she put into her process actually bought something.

If you knew you would make three sales for every ten prospects you put into your process, you could quit worrying about that "one account" and begin trusting your process.

You will never know which prospect will buy. Things happen. The prospect you've cultivated takes a position at another company, or his company is purchased by another company whose purchasing offices are not in your territory. You can't predict these things. You can only trust that if you have ten prospects in your process, some of them will make it all the way through and buy something.

Then, take every prospect purposefully through your process.

Beginning the 16-Step Process— Steps 1 and 2

Looking at this 16-step process makes the various steps you have to complete to close a sale obvious. In Step 1, you identify the company you plan to approach. Next for Step 2, you need a person's name. You can get this name from a Web site, the annual report, or the receptionist. You need a name and phone number. Once you know whom you want to see, you can use the seven-step appointment-getting system (Steps 3–9 on the Ten Most Wanted List; all the details are in a later chapter.) When you get an appointment you'll confirm it by fax, e-mail, or postcard. You see the prospect for the first time in Step 10. The purpose of the first appointment is to sell the prospect on your process and not on your product. You keep moving through the steps of your process. Every time you complete a step, you note the date.

In the remaining chapters you will learn the specifics of each step of the process. You'll get a powerful letter you can adapt for Step 5. You'll get a powerful script to use with a receptionist or leave on your prospect's voice mail. You'll get the proposal-writing template to help you with Step 14. These refinements will help you get through to more prospects, book more firm appointments, make a more powerful first impression, and qualify more quickly.

You can learn a lot about how you sell by examining your Ten Most Wanted List. Like the box score of a baseball game, this tool tells you more than just the score. It reveals how the score actually was made.

When you focus on the process, you also spend less time worrying about closing ratios. Instead, you calculate what I call **advancing ratios**. When you reached a decision maker, what percentage of those calls resulted in an initial consultation? What percentage of consultations turned into presentations? What percentage of presentations resulted in a sale?

Trusting the process is liberating, and tracking your progress is motivating. Too many salespeople have come to think of prospecting, cold calling, seeding, initial meetings, presentations, and even follow-up as the necessary "evils" of sales. Dispense with them quickly, they think, and concentrate on the important thing—the close. My attitude is just the opposite: Concentrate on the steps and the close will follow naturally.

New Business Moves Per Week

The Ten Most Wanted List lays out your direct route to sales success. You now know that in order to make one sale, you must simply take one prospect through all sixteen steps of the process. Fill in all sixteen spaces and you have a sale. Chances are you won't move any single prospect sixteen spaces in a week though. So one vital statistic to track is **New Business Moves Per Week.**

To count your New Business Moves Per Week, use red or blue ink on your Ten Most Wanted List to note each step you take. At the end of the week, count them. If you move eight prospects four spaces each, you will have thirty-two New Business Moves. Record that number at the bottom of your Ten Most Wanted List.

Then photocopy your Ten Most Wanted List and begin using that photocopy to track your progress. All the dates you've marked to indicate your progress are now black again. On Monday decide whom you're going to advance through your sales process. As you do, use red or blue ink to note each step you take.

In this way, you can see at a glance which prospects you're actively working and which may be stalled.

The point system is easy. You get ten New Business Moves for sending out ten articles, ten more for sending those ten letters. You get ten more for dialing the phone ten times. Still no sales, if that's all you do. But as you keep moving the ten prospects through your 16-step process on paper, you advance them through your selling process and get closer to making a sale.

Counting your New Business Moves Per Week gives you a way to focus on the positive progress you've made this week. When you understand the sales process, you gain control and confidence. Understanding exactly what you need to do next with each prospect in your process gives the Accidental Salesperson a renewed sense of purpose. Every day.

You could move one prospect fifteen spaces and get a sale, or you could move ten prospects two spaces each, or five prospects three spaces each.

You now understand "the game within the game." You can see where you're going and where you need coaching. You may find that your process is bogged down at a certain place—Step 10, for example. That means you now need coaching or additional reading on the approach and involvement of a prospect. You don't have a closing problem in this case; you have an opening problem. We can fix that.

By putting down the date you accomplished a step, you build in a sense of urgency for the next move. You also learn how long, on average, it takes to move a prospect through your process.

Once you understand that it takes ten prospects in process to get four presentations and close 75 percent of those, you begin to trust your process. You don't have to worry about that one account closing. You can sell like you already have made your quota, because you are going to make your quota.

Think about that for just a moment. Have you ever noticed how much easier it is to sell once you've made your quota or goal? There are five reasons this is true:

1. You are under no pressure to close this sale and can therefore relax and go with the flow. You don't have to pressure the prospect or yourself.

2. You project a lot more confidence in what you are doing. When you don't absolutely have to have this sale, you come across as an already successful salesperson. And people like doing business with confident, successful salespeople.

3. You are negotiating from a position of strength. You say "This is the price" instead of "I'll run your request for that discount past my sales manager."

4. You can be there for the prospect instead of being there for your grocery money.

5. You are having fun and the prospect senses that you're glad to be there. This is a powerful force for success.

The Ten Most Wanted List gives you a formulaic approach to taking prospects through your entire sales process. It's a proven power tool, with precedents in law enforcement. The FBI employs thousands and spends billions to carry out various investigations. Still, one of the FBI's most famous programs is the "Ten Most Wanted List." Your prospects aren't criminals but they can be almost as elusive. It feels like they bolt out the back door and hide from your phone calls.

If you are serious about selling, you must put many prospects into play.

At the Waterford Crystal factory, we went through every step in the process and paid full retail at the gift shop. Taking your prospects through your process takes the mystery out of higher prices.

Some salespeople balk at the idea that they should have

a system and keep on applying that system over and over, even though it works.

Comedian Ernie Kovaks said, "There is a classic formula for success in the entertainment industry. Beat it to death if it works." More than 250,000 people tour the Waterford Crystal factory every year and all 250,000 of them go through the same tour I went through. Beat it to death if it works.

If you want to see how following formulas can be successful, may I suggest some $2 Sales Training Videos. Try *Rocky, Rocky II, Rocky III, Rocky IV,* and *Rocky V.* Rent *Rambo: First Blood; Rambo: First Blood II;* or *Rambo III.* If you still don't believe in formulas, rent *Back to the Future, Back to the Future II,* or *Back to the Future III.* Same stars, same characters, same stories. Beat it to death if it works.

Speaking of death, let's look at one of the great formulaic programs of all times. You don't even have to rent it. It's still on in syndication. Consult your local listings for the station and time in your area and watch a . . .

Free Sales Training Video
Murder She Wrote (any episode)[1]

Angela Lansbury stars as mystery writer Jessica Fletcher in *Murder She Wrote.* Early in every show one person infuriates several of his or her associates. Within the first fifteen minutes several people reveal a motive to kill this person. Twenty-five minutes into the show someone finds "the body."

Jessica Fletcher just happens to be near where the murder occurs, whether it's in Cabot Cove, Maine; New York; or Los Angeles. One Sunday I turned to Sarah and said, "Why do people invite her anywhere?"

"Jessica, would you like to come to our college and teach a class on creative writing?" She accepts and someone dies in the college gym.

"Jessica, would you please come to our daughter's wedding?" Someone turns up facedown in the hotel swimming pool during the reception.

Ms. Fletcher just happens to be near where the murder occurs. She investigates the murder scene to the dismay of the local detective. Sooner or later, the local cop figures out that this woman is a better detective than he is. They work together on the case. In the last five minutes they confront the murderer, who confesses everything in vivid detail (without being read any rights).

Then there are the previews for the next week's show, which is a variation of the show you just saw.

That show was in the top ten for eleven years!

Like *Murder She Wrote,* the Ten Most Wanted List is a formulaic approach. Like the Waterford Crystal tour, the Ten Most Wanted List takes people through every step in your sales process.

You now have a crystal clear concept of your sales process.

Note

1. *Murder She Wrote.* 1984–. Produced by Peter S. Fisher in collaboration with Richard Levinson and William Link. Universal TV [CBS]. Television broadcast.

Chapter 6

Why You Must Quit Making "Sales Calls"

This is the first book on selling successfully that has ever advised salespeople to quit making sales calls.

I'll let you in on a little secret. There are "Accidental Sales Managers" who upon being promoted become proponents of their salespeople making more sales calls than **they** ever made. It's something they can measure, and that makes them feel more in control.

Ludwig Borne said, "Getting rid of a delusion makes us wiser than getting hold of a truth."

Accidental Salespeople delude themselves by calling nearly everything they do a "sales call."

For years sales managers have asked their reports, "How many calls did you make today?" Their reports tell them what they want to hear. They do this by calling everything they do a sales call. They delude themselves and their sales managers into believing they are being productive when they may merely be busy.

When you sell on purpose, you understand that selling is about two things:

1. Making a face-to-face proposal to a qualified prospect, and
2. Getting into position to make a face-to-face proposal to a qualified prospect.

Making any move that doesn't help you accomplish one of those two objectives is wasted motion.

Dartnell's 29th Sales Force Compensation Survey 1996–1997 tells us that today's salesperson makes fewer than three "calls" per day.[1] That statistic, although revealing, still doesn't tell us everything we need to know to be successful. Does it mean you should knock off at noon if you already have seen three prospects?

When I was selling, I realized that making fewer calls with higher quality could result in more business. But I didn't have a way to justify that approach to my sales manager, whose mantra was: "The more doors you open, the more sales you close."

The Chart is one way to look at the quality issue.

(Not long ago, I was discussing this concept of not calling everything you do a sales call with some British sales managers. They gave me a new term to consider. A "sighting" is when you "see a prospect at a soccer game, make eye contact, and wave.")

"Quit making calls." Not the sort of sales advice you expect from a book that purports to tell you how to sell more. But it's sound advice. I vividly recall the day I came to that conclusion.

I had been retained as a sales consultant for a firm that needed one. I asked to see the systems and tools already in place so I could understand the process already in place.

"Here are the call (that word again) reports for last week. My salespeople are making a lot of calls but they're not closing anything," the sales manager said worriedly. "Maybe I should make them make **more** calls."

Although making more calls seems to be a reasonable solution to any sales problem, many misguided sales managers mistake a flurry of activity for real productivity.

After reading several reports, I came to this entry:

The sales rep had entered this description of his latest meeting with a prospect. It read, "Stopped by XYZ company. Ed (the contact) was out. He was having lunch with a vendor at Happy Joe's Pizza. Will **call again** tomorrow."

I read it again in disbelief. Why document something that did nothing to advance the sales process, I wondered.

When I asked the salesperson why he had taken the time

to document what clearly was a wasted effort, he said, "We are required to make a minimum of five calls a day and that was one of them." By calling everything he did a call, he was fooling himself and his manager into thinking he was doing his job.

One salesperson in this same company had entered in her call report, "Dropped off coffee mug as a gift." Chalk up another "call." Only four more to go and she could go home feeling good about how hard she worked. (Or could she?)

That was the beginning of my crusade to get salespeople to call what they do **what it is**. When all you have to measure is the number of "calls," you get an inaccurate view of what it is you're really doing. Making the calls becomes the requirement instead of making sales. When you quit counting calls, you can start counting the things that count.

Greek orator and statesman Demosthenes said, "Nothing is easier than self-deceit. For what each man wishes, that he also believes to be true."

To sell on purpose you must be brutally honest with yourself about what you are really doing. You do a lot of things to get in position to make a proposal. I like Intel CEO Andy Grove's idea of looking at the different tasks you perform as "outputs." Not all of your outputs have the same value, although they might all be necessary.

Let's look at some possible outputs and label them. Adapt these "truth in sales labeling" laws and you will never again call anything you do a sales call.

Here are seven sales outputs I recommend you start counting today:

1. *Seeds.* The number of articles on business issues you send or fax to a customer. For every article you send to a legitimate prospect, you count one "seed."

2. *Letters.* Any introductory letter, thank you note, or letter to clarify a point counts as one letter.

3. *Dials.* If you dial the phone to try to reach a prospect or customer, you get one dial. Dialing the phone may or may not result in a contact, but you have to start somewhere.

4. *Contacts.* If you accidentally (just kidding) get put through to the person you are dialing or if that person picks up his or her own extension, you get one contact. You can get a dial without a contact, but you can't get a contact without a dial unless you are knocking on doors.

5. *Appointments booked.* If you dial the phone, contact the person you want to talk with, and book an appointment, you get one appointment booked.

6. *Customer Needs Analyses conducted.* If you have a meeting with a prospect that results in an exchange of information and needs, you get one Customer Needs Analysis. This could include taking a tour of your prospect's facility.

7. *Proposals.* You present a solution and ask for an order for a specific amount of money—and you have made one proposal.

The proposal is the most important output you can make. The first six outputs help put you in position to make the proposal.

At the end of the day, you count your outputs. Your scenario might look like this: You go to the office in the morning and send out five seeds, write two letters, dial the phone ten times, make three contacts, book one appointment. Then you leave the office and meet with three prospects. At those meetings you do two Customer Needs Analyses, and make one proposal.

You had twenty-four different outputs. You did not make twenty-four sales calls.

Accidental Salesperson Axiom:
Calling what you do exactly what it is is a
powerful force for success.

Corollary:
In counting the things that count, you establish ratios to make
the right decisions about the activities you need to
do more or less of.

The famous exchange in our next $2 Sales Training Video speaks to many Accidental Salespeople:

"You can't handle the truth."

Too many salespeople don't deal well with the harsh reality of selling. While *A Few Good Men* is a courtroom drama, it is also about taking your job seriously. Let's watch:

$2 Sales Training Video
A Few Good Men[2]

At their base in Guantanamo Bay, Cuba, two Marines have broken into William Santiago's room and assaulted him. Santiago dies.

In Washington, D.C., Lieutenant Daniel Kaffee (played by Tom Cruise) is chosen to defend Santiago's assailants at their court martial. Fresh out of Harvard Law School, he is a relatively lazy Naval attorney. During the past nine months he has handled forty-four cases by plea bargain. Joanne Calloway (Demi Moore) is Kaffee's superior officer. She wants the case herself, but her superior officers assign it to Kaffee, assuming he will plea bargain it away.

When Kaffee shows up unprepared, Calloway says, "You're going to have to go deeper than that. My job is to make sure that you do your job."

Kaffee knows his clients are guilty of the assault. Defending them is made more difficult because they refuse to rat on their superior officers. Kaffee must somehow prove that they were following orders instead of initiating the assault on their own. Kaffee and his team suspect that Colonel Nathan Jessup (Jack Nicholson's character) has ordered the "Code Red." Code Red is an informal form of internal discipline. The troops themselves issue the discipline as the commanding officers look away. It's an off-the-books, illegal, and highly effective form of keeping the troops in line.

The problem is they have no evidence and no witnesses on which to build a case other than the testimony of the accused soldiers, who finally admit that Lieutenant Kendrick issued them the order to give Santiago a Code Red.

As he walks out of the courtroom after entering a surprise plea of "not guilty" for his clients, Kaffee turns, takes in the scene, smiles, and says, "So this is what a courtroom looks like." You can see him begin to take this case seriously. He also is wrestling with the legacy of his father, a brilliant trial attorney whose shoes he fears he might not be good enough to fill.

The defense attorneys prepare for the trial like Rocky prepared to fight Apollo Creed. They work twenty-hour days for three weeks running. Kaffee tells his team, "This is about a sales pitch. It's not about the law. It's going to be won by the lawyers."

In the climactic scene, Danny Kaffee calls Colonel Jessup as a witness and asks a series of questions that goad him into admitting that he ordered the illegal Code Red.

Jessup tells Kaffee, "We follow orders, son. We follow orders, or people die. It's that simple. Are we clear?"

"Crystal," says Kaffee.

Kaffee says, "If Lieutenant Kendrick gave an order that Santiago wasn't to be touched, then why did he have to be transferred?"

"You want answers."

"I want the truth."

"You can't handle the truth. You don't want the truth because you want me on that wall." And (in a wonderful piece of acting) Colonel Jessup slowly snaps.

As he melts down he admits that he, in fact, did issue a Code Red and in doing so indicts himself. Had he not, Kaffee could have been court-martialed for falsely accusing Jessup of conduct unbecoming an officer.

A Few Good Men offers two hours of great performances and four powerful lessons on selling.

1. *The time spent doing research and preparing questions can give you a compelling competitive advantage.* Digging deeper to find more facts than the prosecutor helped win the case.

2. *Setting solid objectives is a key to success.* Kaffee was clear that all he had to do was prove his clients were carrying out orders. He kept that fact foremost in his mind and relentlessly pursued the proof.

3. *Visual aids can help you sell.* In a surprise move, two uniformed officers walk into the courtroom, ostensibly to testify on a critical piece of evidence Jessup tried to cover up. Although they never testify, their silent presence has an interesting effect on the outcome of the trial.

4. *Take your job seriously.* You can handle the truth. In fact, the only way to sell on purpose is to tell yourself and your sales manager exactly what is going on.

"Quit making calls" is a startling statement. It is meant to get you to conduct a daily reality check on just how well you are doing. Counting the things that count is critical. Tracking the things that keep your career on track helps you make better decisions on how you are using your time.

In this "Age of Interruptions" it is increasingly easy to get mired in minutiae. Think about the technology that steals our focus. Fax machines, e-mail, voice mail, cellular phones, and pagers conspire to keep us from completing our high-payoff projects.

"Beep-elepsy" is the new epidemic. Trying to focus on your customer as your beeper or cell phone vibrates is very difficult. Your eyes glaze over and your attention is splintered. Even if your customer doesn't notice, you miss what the customer is saying. That's crucial.

"Got-a-minute" meetings usually consume at least twenty.

You never seem to be finished. You go home when you are tired, not when your work is completed. Most people today have two hundred to three hundred hours of unfinished projects, one source estimates. If you can confront the fact that you can't get it all done, you may get the more important things done.

People still buy from salespeople, but prospects are increasingly harder to see. Every move in this book is designed so that the prospect will want to see you.

On NFL broadcasts, you'll often hear a commentator talk about "time of possession." When one team controls the ball for a significantly longer period of time than the other, that team usually wins.

You can easily measure your Time Spent Selling (see Figure 6-1). For one solid week count only the minutes and hours you spend in front of a decision maker. It doesn't matter whether you are conducting a needs analysis or making a proposal. What matters is face-to-face time versus windshield time or computer time.

Have you ever gone home after a long day and been greeted by these words, "Hi, honey. How was your day?" If your answer was that you put out one fire after the other, join the club. You are a salesperson, not a firefighter. You are supposed to be in the field, not in the office.

Time Spent Selling is an important statistic to keep track of. Because there is direct correlation between seeing your prospects and making sales, your Time Spent Selling number tells you exactly how to increase your income: Increase the number.

Putting in time on the job is not what selling is all about. Time Spent Selling is the essential measurement of how productive you really are.

Time spent on these things doesn't count:

Flying
Driving
Waiting in lobbies
Writing reports
Sleeping in hotels
Checking your e-mail, voice mail, snail mail
Reading memos from your boss
Attending sales meetings
Being trained on the new software
Picking up your laundry
Taking your dog to the vet

Figure 6-1. Measuring the time you spend face-to-face with customers will give you instant feedback on how to increase your sales.

Time Spent Selling

Month

	Mon	Tues	Wed	Thur	Fri	Sat
AM						
PM						
AM						
PM						
AM						
PM						
AM						
PM						
AM						
PM						

Total $ Sales This Month	
÷ Total Hours in Front of Clients	
= $ Value of Face-to-Face Time	

Total Compensation This Month	
÷ Total Hours in Front of Clients	
= $ "Hourly Wage"	

There are so many things that eat up time and distract from the real purpose of selling, it's a wonder we sell anything at all. I challenge you to log the hours you spend in front a customer for one week. The next week, try to increase that by fifteen minutes.

Nothing matters more than Time Spent Selling. You are worth more in the field than at the fax machine. And, although you should not neglect reading and paperwork, they should not cause you to ignore your customer.

To use the Time Spent Selling log, just time every face-to-face client interaction and enter the number of minutes or hours you were with customers or prospects. You can get a more accurate reading with an inexpensive stopwatch. One of the fastest ways to increase your sales is to increase your Time Spent Selling. Use the form I've included here, or keep track on the pages of whatever time management system you're using (e.g., Day-Timers®).

You now have seven outputs to track and the Ten Most Wanted List to track them on. You also have a new power tool, the Time Spent Selling log. These reality checks will give you feedback and keep you permanently focused on selling on purpose.

Notes

1. Christian P. Heide. *Darnell's 29th Sales Force Compensation Survey 1996–1997* (Chicago: The Dartnell Corporation, 1996).
2. *A Few Good Men.* 1992. Directed by Rob Reiner. 138 minutes. Castle Rock Entertainment, Columbia Pictures Corporation. Videocassette.

Part 3

Doing Everything Better

The Systematic Approach to Every Step in Your Process

Accidental Sales Training Seminar
Airport Salesperson

It is July is 13, 1995. I am sitting in the deli at the Minne-apolis–St. Paul airport having a late lunch when the seminar starts. Without fanfare, the teacher enters the room. He is wearing jeans and a T-shirt. He is not dressed for success by our standards. Instead of a briefcase, there is a bulging fanny pack cinched around his waist.

He systematically approaches people at every table. He's interrupting their lunch in order to make his sales presentation. In about two minutes, he has made ten presentations. His selling cycle requires one more face-to-face interaction to close. He asks each one of his prospects for an order and closes four out of ten. He collects the money (cash!), stuffs it into his pack, and presumably heads for his next group of prospects.

I sit there in awe, analyzing what I have just seen. In two minutes he has systematically and successfully worked the roomful of frazzled, frequent flyers, closed 40 percent of them, and collected $8 cash! I paid him $2 myself and am now the proud owner of a product I didn't even know I needed.

Having nothing better to do, I do the math on a napkin. Here's the way I worked it out.

$8 in two minutes = $240 per hour

$240 per hour X 8 hours = $1,920 per day

$1,920 per day X 5 days = $9,600 per week

$9,600 per week X 50 weeks = $480,000 per year

All Cash—No Receivables

There are more than twenty restaurants at the airport and more than ninety gates. There is a fresh supply of prospects for this salesperson every sixty to ninety minutes, as new flights land or prepare to take off. I estimate he's getting at least a 100 percent markup on his product. By this point, you may be ready to quit your job and join this salesperson. Before you do, let me tell you the rest of the story.

His product is a set of three screwdrivers, each about two inches long, in a plastic pack that doubles as a key chain. His presentation is written on a card slightly larger than a standard business card. It reads:

HELLO! I AM A DEAF PERSON. I'M OFFERING YOU THIS HANDY TOOL KEY CHAIN, WHICH MAY BE USED FOR GLASSES, WATCHES, COMPUTERS, AND MORE FOR ONLY $2.00. THE PROCEEDS HELP PAY MY EDUCATIONAL AND LIVING EXPENSES. MAY I INTEREST YOU IN ONE? "MAY GOD BLESS YOU! THANKS FOR YOUR KINDNESS!"

The illustration on the card is the American Sign Language sign for "I love you."

After putting a set of screwdrivers and his card on my table, the salesperson moved to each table in the room and repeated the process. When he came back to "close" the sale, he looked at his product and then looked at me, raised his eyebrow, turned his palm face up, and communicated this question: "Well, are you going to buy it?" I handed him my $2 and he signed "thank you" and moved on.

I watched as some people shook their heads in the universal sign for "No, I'm not." When they did he smiled, picked up what could have been their set of screwdrivers, and moved on to the next table and repeated the same process.

I spent $2 for a set of screwdrivers, and I gained seven free lessons about selling. That's value added.

1. *Tell people about yourself early.* Establish who you are and why they should buy from you. A little self-disclosure reveals that you're a human being and not just a selling machine. It could be as simple as using the Magic Phrase, "In preparing for this meeting I . . ." or something a bit more elaborate: "I am a deaf person. I am offering you . . ."

2. *Recover quickly from rejection and move on.* This salesperson got six Nos on his way to his 40 percent closing ratio. He just picked up his screwdriver set and moved on to the next table. He didn't take a break to lick his wounds. He didn't go to the bar to drown his sorrows. He didn't stop at the Caribou Coffee stand to have a cappuccino. He didn't convene a meeting of his fellow screwdriver salespeople to tell them how difficult the job is. He went directly to the next prospect and asked that prospect to buy. He kept right on selling.

I wonder, does this screwdriver salesperson handle rejection well because he has the potential to sell $19,200 a week, or does he have the potential to sell $19,200 a week because he handles rejection well and keeps selling?

The answer, of course, is "Yes."

3. *Respect your product and your prospects will too.* While he moved quickly, he carefully placed each screwdriver set on the table. He did that deliberately, with great care.

4. *Written presentations can help you make a strong case.* This particular salesperson relied on his written presentation. It didn't give every detail, but it made a compelling case for his product. His written presentation laid out the benefits and not just the features. "These screwdrivers may be used for glasses, watches, computers . . ." Sell what the product does and not just what it is. Having the screwdriver set helped me recently when a seminar participant needed to fix her glasses.

5. *Talking is an overrated selling skill.* This salesperson never said a word and still closed 40 percent of the prospects he approached. Salespeople who can talk often overuse this ability. Listening is a vital selling skill. You can listen with your eyes as well as your ears. The deaf salesperson made solid eye contact and read his clients.

6. *You can sell without pagers, cellular telephones, laptop computers, faxes, the Internet, or complicated closing lines.* You can sell more by seeing more people and asking more of them to do business with you. You need to boil down who you are and what you sell to its essence and then go make those presentations.

7. *Find a selling system that works and beat it to death.* Put your system on the line so you don't have to put yourself on the line every day. It may be boring to make that same pitch and sell that same set of screwdrivers to person after person, but could you live on $19,200 a week?

You have a more complex sales process (at least sixteen steps) and a more expensive product to sell than the screwdriver salesperson. However, you can still benefit from having a systematic (automatic) way to move purposefully through each step. In this section you will get refinements to help you take control of the dynamics of every client interaction.

Chapter 7

Getting in to See Anybody

Steps 3–9 in Your Process

The screwdriver salesperson can afford to make cold calls. He works the airport and sells an impulse item.

You can't get in an airplane and start cold calling. So generally the first time you speak with a prospect will be on the telephone. That telephone call won't be the first time you contact the prospect, however.

The screwdriver salesperson has a systematic approach to selling that ensures his success. He has a process he can trust. Of course, you have at least sixteen steps in your selling process, not two. That complicates matters so much that we need to simplify every step in your process.

"Don't Speak to Strangers"

Your early childhood conditioning is the foundation of call reluctance. What was good advice when you were three years old can be a career killer now that you're in sales. You've got to speak to strangers. At the same time, I know calling people out of the blue is daunting. It is much easier to pick up the phone and talk to a person who knows who you are and wants to talk to you than to call a stranger and try to start a conversation.

Not only is it hard for salespeople to make cold calls. Your problem is compounded because your prospects' parents told **them** not to speak to strangers either.

In the past, prospects have defended themselves by placing "gatekeepers" in our paths. Increasingly, they use voice mail to screen out unwanted calls from strangers. Don't worry. By completing Steps 3, 4, and 5 (see Figure 7-1), you separate yourself from the pack of salespeople cold calling your prospects. You already will have had three (count 'em) Level 3 "moments" before you even dial the phone. Your prospects will know your name and why you are calling when they pick up the phone.

You won't be a stranger. They will want to talk with you.

Obviously, when a prospect calls you and asks for a meeting, you have no need for Steps 3–9. You already have booked the first appointment (Step 10). For the rest of your prospects, you will need Steps 3–9.

Step 3: Your First Level 3 "Moment"

Mail or fax your prospect an article about an issue or trend in his or her business. Here's the concept: Market yourself and your company as a resource and not just another vendor. Clip an article from a business newspaper, business magazine, or trade magazine and attach your business card to it. Write something like this on your business card: "Al, Wanted to make sure you saw this. Chris." Or, "Mary, Thought of you when I read this. Chris." Then mail the actual clipping to the prospect. A clipping from *The Wall Street Journal* or an industry trade publication has even more impact than a photocopy (see Figures 7-2 and 7-3).

There is a faster way to do this. Paste the article onto the template (shown in Figure 3-1), put your name and your company's logo on the sheet, and fax the article to the prospect. You can write the same notes on the sheet.

Send short articles (one paragraph, one column, one page tops). While your competitors are inundating your prospects with product literature, price lists, and spec sheets, you

Figure 7-1. By doing steps 3, 4, and 5, you make it more likely that the first phone call will be taken or returned.

Ten Most Wanted List

The 16-Step Selling Process Box Score

Based on your own selling cycle, set a time frame to accomplish all 16 steps.

1. Identify businesses (prospects/clients)
2. Identify decision maker
3. Seed (describe)
4. Seed (describe)
5. Letter
6. Dial
7. Contact decision maker
8. Book first appointment
9. Confirm the first appointment
10. Complete 1st app't; Sell your process & frame the issue
11. Book Customer Needs Analysis
12. Complete Customer Needs Analysis
13. Book the proposal
14. Write the proposal
15. Make the proposal
16. Confirm the order (close)

Totals

Decision makers ID'd ÷ total prospects		Contacts ÷ dials	App'ts confirmed ÷ app't's booked	CNA booked ÷ 1st app't completed	Proposals booked ÷ CNAs	Proposals made ÷ prop's written	Sales closed ÷ prospects started
% Decision makers ID'd		% Reached	% App'ts conf'd	% CNAs booked	% Prop's booked	% Prop's made	Gross Closing Ratio
	Dials ÷ decision makers ID'd	App't's booked ÷ contacts	1st app't completed ÷ app't's confirmed	CNAs completed ÷ CNAs booked	Prop's written ÷ prop's booked	Sales closed ÷ prop's made	
	% Decision makers dialed	% App't's booked	% App't's completed	% CNAs completed	% Prop's written	% Closed	

Figure 7-2.   Send an article and attach your business card.

Mary – Info I thought
you should see.

Bernie Harris
2001 S. Howard Street
Belmont MT 87293
ph 719-234-8997, ext 433
fax 719-234-8999
bharris@aol.com

Atlas Earthmovers
Moving mountains, molehills, and everything in between

T he mitigation of liability is a criin the design and construction
and landscapes for public use. As
becomes increasingly suit-consc
cal and fatal personal injuries will
millions to the budgets of business and agencie
directly trace consumer, patron and user safety
open spaces, commons and other assembly prop
the implementation of grounds-management po
procedure, and to the personnel, supervisors and
ing board or policy makers responsible for them

The amount of money allocated to
safety is an indication of the priority it
has in an organization. However, to
make the most of funds provided for
safety, policy makers need to first
examine the applications of safety in
the care of grounds that the public
uses. The safety of the public or patron
includes the categories of *health, se-
curity* and *well-being*.

Health

Patron health is relevant in a couple
of ways. First, health is achieved
through the prevention of disease or
sickness through *personal hygiene*.
Second, health is achieved through
the prevention of disease or sickness
with *personnel/occupational and en-
vironmental controls*. Both aspects
of health are extremely important to

Continued on page C 4

Constant awareness of safety—from policy
makers to maintenance workers—is ̃eces-
sary to minimize potential liability in public-
use areas.

^{By} Arthur H. Mittelstaedt Jr., Recreation Safety Institute

*In this suit-happy era, constant aware-
ness of safety by policy makers,
management and workers is a must.*

Reduce
public liability
in landscape design
and construction

November 1998   *Grounds Maintenance*   C 1

Figure 7-3.   Use the template to brand you and your company as sources of information.

TO:		Atlas Earthmovers
FROM:	No. of Pages	

Information about business issues and trends I wanted to be sure you saw.

RESEARCH UPDATE: GOOD FOR THE GOOSE... BAD FOR THE ENVIRONMENT?

Various protective measures have afforded some migratory waterfowl a chance to recoup their numbers. However, wetland habitat is shrinking. The result is that more birds are using less wetlands, creating higher population densities. This is causing some concern with researchers who fear this situation could lead not only to more epidemics of avian diseases but also could damage aquatic ecosystems by overwhelming their ability to absorb nutrients added from bird excretions.

To better understand this problem, researchers from Cornell University and the University of Madison—Wisconsin estimated how much waste geese were depositing in the Bosque del Apache National Wildlife Refuge (near Albuquorque, N.M.). This refuge includes 1,200 acres of wetlands that provide a winter home to about 45,000 geese. Adjacent to the wetlands are alfalfa and corn fields (planted specifically for the birds). The researchers discovered that the geese spent most of their time in just one section of the wetlands (where they roosted) and estimated that they deposited around 40 percent (20,000 pounds) of the nitrogen and 75 percent (2,400 pounds) of the phosphorus that entered this wetland during the study. The study lasted one winter.

While the researchers don't think that this amount poses an immediate threat to the wetland, it is of concern because waterfowl populations still are increasing at many wetland sites. Should bird populations begin to damage wetlands habitat, it would create a difficult management problem. Geese and other waterfowl are notoriously difficult to disperse, and creating additional wetlands to accommodate the increasing bird populations would mean obtaining increasingly scarce water resources.

This type of situation should sound familiar to superintendents. Many golf courses attract geese due to their ponds and large swaths of edible turf. Considering the amount of nutrients that geese can deposit into a body of water, it's possible that they could negatively impact pond-water quality—not that superintendents need more reasons to keep geese away.

Research shows that geese can deposit substantial amounts of nitrogen and phosphorus in wetlands. This could affect water quality in ponds adjacent to turf areas.

November 1998   *Grounds Maintenance*   1

Atlas Earthmovers
Moving mountains, molehills,

Bernie Harris
2001 S. Howard Street
Belmont MT 87293
ph 719-234-8997, ext 433
fax 719-234-8999
bharris@aol.com

are quietly establishing yourself as someone who understands and cares about their business and respects their time.

(As you may already have realized, this template is a great way to keep your name in front of your current customers as well!)

By "seeding" the prospect this way you accomplish three things:

1. You make certain that your first move is a Level 3 Moment by providing information of value.

2. You have demonstrated that you are on top of the issues and trends in the prospect's industry. (You did read the article before you sent it, didn't you?)

3. You've put your name (via business card or fax) in front of the prospect for the first time.

Step 4: Repeat Step 3 (Optional)

Two or three days later find another article. Clip it. Attach your business card and mail it or affix the article to the Level 3 template and fax it. This second "seed" reinforces your prospect's first impressions of you as different and noticeably better than the other salespeople who are clamoring for his or her time and attention.

Although advisable, it is not absolutely necessary to complete this step. I suggest you test it. Send five prospects on your Ten Most Wanted List a second seed. Send five just the first seed and go right to Step 5. See if adding the additional step gains you a higher percentage of contacts and appointments, and then decide for yourself if this extra step is worth it to you. Whatever you do, don't skip Step 5.

Step 5: Send "The Letter"

Let two business days pass and mail "The Letter" (see Figure 7-4). In fact, I strongly suggest that you get this letter into your word processor and into your mail-merge system now.

The Letter is tested and proven. It works.

Figure 7-4. The Letter.

3000 Cahill Main • Madison, WI 53711 USA
608.274.0400 • 800.255.9853 • fax 608.274.1400 • www.lytleorganization.com
Sales offices: Sydney, Australia • Tijuana, Mexico (San Ysidro, California)

[Date]

[Name and Title]
[Company Name]
[Inside address line 3]
[Inside address line 4]

Dear [Name],

Management is a series of interruptions
that are constantly being interrupted by more interruptions.

That's why the reading time on this letter is 27 seconds.

When you meet with me, the presentation is brief and preplanned. It's also client-focused. I want you to remember our meeting as a positive, information-packed experience—not as an interruption.

I will call you on [Day] morning to ask you to meet with me for 25 minutes. This is a non-decision-making, fact-finding meeting.

Good secretaries screen decision makers from interruptions. Voice-mail systems let you pick and choose which callers get some of your limited time.

When you meet with me, I will be presenting information that will help [Company name] [Benefit, e.g., improve its profits]. Thanks in advance for not treating my call like an interruption.

Sincerely,

[Name]
[Title]

Our Mission: To create and deliver sales and management products, processes and systems that make successful people more successful

Step 5A: Schedule the Time to Make the Phone Call You Just Promised to Make

That goes without saying, but I'm saying it anyway. The Letter works for four reasons:

1. It tells the prospect what you are going to do (dial the phone) and builds more credibility when you keep your promise and call when you said you would.
2. It does not require the prospect to return your call. You're just asking the prospect to alert his or her secretaries that you will be calling. In fairness, then, the prospect must give your letter some consideration.
3. It prepares the prospect for your telephone call. And . . .
4. It contains a "Magic Phrase."

Magic Phrase
"This is a non-decision-making, fact-finding meeting."

Accidental Sales Training Seminar
Free Information

I have replied to an ad that offers free information to people who are interested in exploring a unique business opportunity.

The company, as promised, sends me a free cassette tape. I am now a lead.

After a reasonable amount of time, a salesperson from the company follows up. She invites me to take the next step in his process, which is to attend a seminar for interested and qualified prospects to learn more about the opportunity.

I resist.

"Chris," she assures me, "this session lays out the opportunity and is the only way for you to really know if there's a fit. And I promise you, this is a non-decision-making, fact-finding visit."

I quit resisting and attend the meeting.

That magic phrase worked on me for the same reason it will work on your prospects. It positions the first meeting as less threatening and reduces the prospect's need to resist. Use "This is a non-decision-making, fact-finding meeting" in your letters and when you contact the prospect on the phone. Discover how many more appointments you land by letting customers feel secure about meeting with you.

This is the letter our own salespeople use to get prospects to take their calls. Customers have commented that the only reason they agreed to meet with our salespeople was The Letter. In fact, a sales manager for a billion-dollar company asked if he could copy The Letter and let his salespeople use it to get appointments with their prospects.

You now have made three powerful and positive impressions that ensure you are not a stranger when prospects talk to you for the first time.

Step 6: Dial the Phone

You have told the prospect in writing that you are going to phone on a certain day. Dial the phone. You may reach the client directly. More likely, a secretary or voice-mail system will pick up.

The secretary will say, "Good morning, XYZ Company, this is Heidi."

Now it's your turn to talk. Use this format. "Hello, Heidi. John Keating, please. This is Chris Lytle calling."

Either you will be put through or you will hear those eight wonderful words, "May I tell him what this is regarding?"

Most Accidental Salespeople dread those eight words. When you're selling on purpose you welcome them. You now have a tremendous opportunity to separate yourself from the pack.

This is the combination of words that unlocks the vault that gatekeepers guard and gets many of them to put you right through.

(Smiling) "Sure. He just had a letter from me. I'm following up. John is expecting my call, and I promised I'd call this morning."

Notice how much stronger that is than saying, "Yes, I represent ACME Widget and I'd like to set up a meeting to show him our new line."

Say those words with a smile and confidence in your voice. Expect to be put through. In many cases you will be. The articles and The Letter that preceded this call have done their work. Other times the prospect will be in a meeting, on another line, or away from the office.

You may be put through to the prospect or the prospect's voice mail. In either case, here is what you say.

"Hello, John. This is Chris Lytle. John, you just had a letter from me. I've also sent you a couple of articles. When is a convenient time for us to get together for a twenty-five-minute, non-decision-making, fact-finding meeting? Would a week from tomorrow work for you, say 9:20?" (If you're talking to voice mail, you can add, "Again, this is Chris Lytle at 608-274-0400, ext. 323. Thank you.").

The key concept is to ask for the appointment next week. This communicates that you are busy and that you plan ahead. If you ask for an appointment this afternoon or tomorrow morning, you send the opposite message. Prospects want to work with busy, successful salespeople. If you're not booked in advance, you're not busy. Therefore, you're not successful—at least in the prospect's mind.

Another reason to ask for the appointment next week is that the prospect is already swamped. Management is a series of interruptions that are constantly being interrupted by more interruptions. Ask for an appointment today or tomorrow and the prospect can answer truthfully, "I'm swamped. Call me in thirty days."

Asking for the appointment next week or even two weeks

from today lets the prospect plan that day around your visit instead of trying to squeeze you in right away.

Booking the appointment for next week also gives you an opportunity to take the next step . . . Step 9.

Step 9: Confirm the Appointment

As soon as you book the appointment, skip to Step 9. You don't have to go through all the steps once the prospect has agreed to meet with you. You can confirm the appointment by postcard, fax, or e-mail. Figure 7-5 is a sample appointment confirmation postcard.

Confirming the appointment is one more impression you make before you meet the prospect face-to-face. It will go into the "file" (mental or otherwise) the prospect is keeping on you.

It is possible that the prospect may resist meeting with you. This happens despite your Level 3, professional, systematic approach. The most important thing to keep in mind is that you are not trying to sell the prospect your product or

Figure 7-5. It's a nice touch to confirm appointments. You're hard to forget.

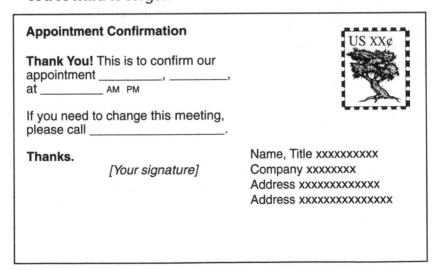

Appointment Confirmation

Thank You! This is to confirm our appointment _____, _____, at _____ AM PM

If you need to change this meeting, please call _____.

Thanks.
                    [Your signature]

US XX¢

Name, Title xxxxxxxxxx
Company xxxxxxx
Address xxxxxxxxxxxx
Address xxxxxxxxxxxxxx

service right now. The purpose of this contact is to sell the appointment. Avoid getting trapped into making your presentation.

You sell the appointment on the phone and sell your product face-to-face. If there is resistance, you can use these scripts to handle it:

Your prospect might politely decline by saying, "I appreciate your call, but my budget is already allocated."

Your answer: "I understand. I don't know if we should be doing business or not, John. At the same time, I have some information that can help you right now. I make it a practice to meet people whom I'd like to meet and whom I may be able to help now or in the future. I'll ask some questions and listen. In any case, it's a non-decision-making, fact-finding meeting. I wonder if we could get together next Thursday?"

Your prospect may not outright reject you, but may be incredibly indifferent to your phone call. "I'm just not interested right now."

Your response: "I understand, and at the same time I'm willing to risk a trip and a twenty-five-minute meeting because I have many customers who at first told me that they weren't interested either. I first had to demonstrate how they could get bottom-line results. Can we get together anyway?"

If you use one or two of these scripts the prospect may even say something like, "You're awfully pushy."

Your response: "John, I sent you two articles, I wrote you a letter, and now I'm asking you to meet with me to see if there is a need for what I sell. I've worked with a lot of companies and helped them improve their profits. I hope you'll agree that I am persisting professionally instead of being pushy. Can we get together?"

If you are talking with a CEO or top management person, you can add this question: "Don't you wish your company's salespeople would approach prospects and persist the way I do?"

Said with humor in the tone of your voice, that question

can be a real icebreaker. A typical response is, "I sure do. Do you want a job?"

Generally top management wants its salespeople to be assertive and go after business just the way you are.

Handle the resistance, and if the prospect says he doesn't want to meet with you a third time, say "Thank you. Goodbye."

You do not want to get into an argument the first time you speak with a prospect. You want to leave an impression that you are persistent but polite. It is critical that you don't take the rejection personally. Here's what Accidental Salespeople have to internalize in order to succeed:

Accidental Salesperson Axiom:
You are not putting yourself on the line when you prospect.

Corollary:
You are putting your prospecting system on the line
and you can always change your system.

Think back to our screwdriver salesperson. He got six "Nos" in two minutes. Now that's rejection! He also made four sales in that time.

He didn't put "himself" on the line. He put his product on the table. He put his card on the table. He put his selling system on the line.

This seven-step appointment-getting system works.

Handling rejection is part of the job. **Preventing** rejection means you'll spend less time handling rejection. This system will prevent a lot of rejection.

Let's step backward now. Suppose you didn't speak with your prospect but left a message.

Step 6A: The Prospect Returns Your Call

When you use this system prospects are more likely to return your call. When they do, you will have a tendency to say

what virtually every salesperson says, "Thank you for returning my call."

Don't say it.

Accidental Salespeople say that. When you sell on purpose, you don't do things accidentally. You use words wisely
to communicate your point of differentiation on every client
interaction. Saying "Thank you for returning my call" implies that very few people return your calls. You are in essence
saying, "This is a surprise. It is extremely kind of you, a powerful businessperson, to return a call to a lowly salesperson
like me."

That's not what you meant to say. So, instead use . . .

Magic Phrase

"Hello, _____. I was expecting your call."

The best thing about saying "I was expecting your call"
is that it's different. It implies that a lot of important people
return your calls because you have something of value to
offer.

The first time you say it you will feel a bit awkward. I
promise you that after you have said it seven times and felt
how much better you feel when you do say it, you will never
go back to "Thanks for returning my call."

When the prospect calls you back, go at once to the script
at Step 6 in your system. "You just had a letter from me and
a couple of articles. When is a convenient time for us to get
together? Would a week from tomorrow work? Say, 9:20?"
Work the resistance. Sell the meeting.

In order for this prospecting system to work, you have to
work it. You will book more appointments on your first contact than ever before. If, for some reason, you don't book an
appointment, there is, of course, a backup system.

Somewhere out there a thousand sales trainers are saying, "Most sales are made after the seventh 'No,' and most
salespeople quit after the second one." This system is designed to give you ways to have at least eight interactions
before you move on to a better prospect.

So if your first phone contact doesn't turn into an appointment wait a week and go to . . .

Step 7: Repeat Step 1— Send Another Article

You want to demonstrate that you haven't given up and that you still believe you have something of value. You can then go to Step 8. You will need to invest a dollar.

Step 8: Send "The Lottery Ticket Letter"

The lottery ticket on the letter is what direct mail experts call a "grabber" (see Figure 7-6). The lottery ticket gets the letter moved from the B pile to the A pile. It grabs the prospect's attention and gets him involved with your mailing. It's irresistible. He has to play the game and scratch off the coating to see if he has won something.

Since many prospects open their mail over the wastebasket, the lottery ticket ensures that the letter will be read, saved, and maybe even shown to colleagues. One salesperson booked seven straight appointments with seven lottery ticket letters. She concluded that it works.

Once you have sent The Lottery Ticket Letter you make the follow-up phone call. Use the same words you use to follow up The Letter.

"Hello. XYZ Company, Heidi speaking."

"Hello, Heidi. John Keating, please. This is Chris Lytle calling."

"May I tell him what this is regarding?"

(Smiling) "Sure, he just had a letter from me. It had a lottery ticket on it. He's expecting my call, and I promised I'd call this morning."

"I'll put you through."

RING. RING.

Figure 7-6.   If the meeting with a prospect is worth a buck to you, send the letter.

3000 Cahill Main • Madison, WI 53711 USA
608.274.0400 • 800.255.9853 • fax 608.274.1400 • www.lytleorganization.com
Sales offices: Sydney, Australia • Tijuana, Mexico (San Ysidro, California)

[Date]

[Name and Title]
[Company Name]
[Inside address line 3]
[Inside address line 4]

Dear [Name],

Take a chance. Meet with me.

I hope this lottery ticket is a big winner. Odds are it won't be, but it's fun to take a chance once in a while.

Some risks are fun to take because they involve a small investment with a potentially big payoff.

When you meet with me, I'll show you a systematic approach to [the problem your product/service solves] that works.

Our business is [Insert your mission statement or slogan if appropriate].

[Name], take a chance. Meet with me for 25 minutes. I promise not to waste a second of your time! I will call you Friday morning to suggest a convenient time.

Sincerely,

[Name]
[Title]

Our Mission: To create and deliver sales and management products, processes and systems that make successful people more successful.

"Hello."

"Hello, John. This is Chris Lytle. You just had a letter from me with a lottery ticket attached. Did you win? (Listen) When is a convenient time for us to get together? Would a week from tomorrow work? Say, 9:20?"

Sending The Lottery Ticket Letter gives you another legitimate reason to call your prospect. The odds of your prospect winning the lottery with the ticket you sent are very low. However, your odds of getting an appointment go up dramatically when you send The Lottery Ticket Letter.

If you've gone through this appointment-getting process and the prospect still hasn't agreed to meet with you, move on to the next prospect.

Just don't quit too soon.

Just as many prospects resist meeting with salespeople, many salespeople resist using scripts and systems.

Choosing your words wisely is part of being a pro. You already use scripts whether you choose to call them that or not. Accidental Salespeople say the same things to different prospects. They use the same openings, tell the same stories. Their openings just have less purpose and, therefore, less power.

This system took me twelve years to research, develop, and test. I didn't work on it full-time, but it represents a major commitment of research and experimentation. You get it in one concise chapter. You can get a card with the whole system printed on two sides if you e-mail us and ask for the "Appointment-Getting Cue Card." (You'll find our e-mail link at www.lytleorganization.com.) Keep the card by your phone and you can approach any prospect with increased confidence because you'll never forget your lines.

It's okay. Pros use scripts. Hey, even David Letterman uses cue cards.

Like Letterman and Leno, you also want to rehearse your lines. You don't want to read your script like a telemarketer selling lightbulbs during the dinner hour. You want to sound natural, and you will, once you have adapted these scripts to your own industry and your own style. If they sound canned, it's only because you haven't practiced and internalized the concepts.

This systematic approach—seeds, letters, phone call, and voice-mail scripts—can multiply your appointment-closing ratio two, three, or more times. It requires a little more work than you may be used to doing. But once you set up the system, the system will set you apart and maybe even set you free.

"Approach and involvement" was rated the number one "must have" selling skill in a survey of more than eight hundred companies employing a total of more than ninety thousand salespeople.[1]

This seven-step appointment-getting system gives you a professional approach. You're not trying to trick people into meeting with you or buying from you. After all, if you were taught the Golden Rule, it will be difficult to do unto others what you wouldn't want them to do unto you.

That's exactly the problem Richard Dreyfuss's character faces at the beginning of *Tin Men.*

$2 Sales Training Video
Tin Men[2]

Tin Men opens in a Cadillac dealership as the salesperson tries to close Dreyfuss's character BB Babowsky on a new, powder-blue Cadillac.

"Well, what do you think?" says the Cadillac salesman.

"Don't press me," BB snaps back. "I really don't want you to hustle me here. You know what I mean. I really . . . I really hate that. I hate being hustled," he tells the car salesperson as he leafs through the full-color brochure on the Cadillac he's ready to buy.

"I just want a nice honest price. You know? I don't want any special deals, just a nice honest price. Am I making myself clear?"

"Of course, Mr. Babowsky. Now," says the car salesperson, picking up pen and order pad, "how much are you willing to pay?"

"You're doing it, see, you're doing it already. You're giving me a hustle number," says BB.

"I'm just trying to get an idea of how much you're willing to pay."

"$4. I'd like to pay $4 a month."

"Now that is not an honest answer," says the salesperson.

"Well, what do you want to hear? Why don't you just tell me what you want me to pay, okay, and then I'll tell you whether I'm willing to pay it. And then we won't have to get this hustle number going, which I really hate. What do I want to pay? I want to pay nothing."

BB has to have a Cadillac, but he doesn't want to be pressured or manipulated into buying one. The irony is that aluminum siding salespeople like BB majored in manipulation and they used unscrupulous tactics to make their sales. In fact, these practices are being investigated by the newly formed Home Improvement Commission as the movie opens.

Shortly, BB Babowsky takes delivery on his new powder-blue Cadillac and backs out of the dealership right into the path of the Cadillac driven by Danny DeVito's character, Ernest Tilley, and the film is off and running.

BB's brand new car has one-sixteenth of a mile on it and already it has a dented left rear fender. The characters played by DeVito and Dreyfuss become instant, bitter enemies.

Ernest Tilley and BB Babowsky are "Tin Men," the high-pressure salespeople who cover up their low self-esteem by buying Cadillacs. They have low self-esteem because they are con men who sell aluminum siding to the unsuspecting citizens of Baltimore.

"Where in the Constitution does it say that you can't hustle someone?" is one way they justify their use of deceptive, high-pressure sales tactics. They will say anything to a customer. In fact, when one of the Tin Men has a heart attack in a customer's living room, it's hard to know whether it's real or just another sales ploy. One legendary Tin Man cut seven inches out of the middle of his yardstick to increase the square footage on the bids he made.

The Tin Men love to spend time at the diner and the bar, talking about the scams they have pulled and the deals they have closed. Still, they understand that building trust with a customer is essential. One of their trust-building techniques is to surreptitiously drop a $5 bill in the living room, where they are having their meeting with the homeowner. They will go over to the $5 bill, pick it up, and hand it to the prospect saying, "This must be yours, because I didn't drop it." Whether the customer takes the $5 bill or tells the salesperson it isn't his, the salesperson has already developed trust. The customer is supposed to think to himself, "Gee, he wouldn't take the $5 bill he found on my floor, so he must be an honest man."

Another approach is to show up at the prospect's front door, set up a camera on the front lawn, and run the *Life* magazine scam. The Tin Men explain to the homeowner, "We need a picture of your house for a layout on how ugly houses are before the aluminum siding is added." The unsuspecting prospect wonders if hers could be the "after" house instead of the "before" house, and the sales pitch begins. After much debate and stalling, the Tin Men allow that it might be possible to make this house the "after" picture but, "We'll have to move fast."

Tin Men is a film about bitter rivals as well as the end of an era in selling. The Home Improvement Commission has placed one of their investigators, posing as an aluminim siding salesman, in Babowsky's company, and he is picking up information about how the scams work. By the end of the film, both Babowsky and Tilley have lost their business licenses and are in the same boat (or at least the same Cadillac), speculating on what they will do next.

An Accidental Salesperson would recoil against the stereotypes presented in *Tin Men*. At the same time, these con men knew a powerful approach was necessary to break preoccupation and involve the customer in the sales process. They also knew they had to build trust early in the relationship because their reputation preceded them. The fact that they chose to build trust by using a dishonest ploy—the $5 bill trick—is one of the reasons they gave selling a bad name.

Tin Men portrays a darker side of selling, but today's salespeople still need strong openings. Some sales trainers call this a startling statement. I was startled when the shoeshine salesperson called out my brand of shoe as I was passing his shoeshine stand at O'Hare Airport. "Let me shine those Cole-Haan shoes for you, sir."

Another approach is to use truisms. A truism is something that instantly gets people to agree with you. Truisms can be trite or biting. Biting is better.

While you can be glad that you'll never have to use unscrupulous tactics, *Tin Men* does teach the power of a strong opening. The Tin Men had tested, proven openings that got them in the door.

If you are going to sell on purpose, you need an approach that works time and time again. It can and should be an honest approach, but it can still be thought-provoking and riveting.

If you've ever "felt funny" about approaching new prospects, be glad you don't have to do like the Tin Men did. You have a whole range of kinder, gentler approaches that also are ethical and effective.

The approach I am talking about is Level 3 touches, with the first letter stating the obvious. "Management is a series of interruptions that are constantly being interrupted by more interruptions." A truism. Truth resonates with people. Think about what other truisms you can use.

Notes

1. Christian P. Heide. *Dartnell's 29th Sales Force Compensation Survey 1996–1997* (Chicago: The Dartnell Corporation, 1996).
2. *Tin Men.* 1987. Directed by Barry Levinson. 112 minutes. Touchstone Pictures. Videocassette.

Chapter 8

What to Do if You "Accidentally" Get an Appointment

Steps 10, 11, and 12

The batter hits the ball sharply to center field. It's going to the wall. Sammy Sosa chases it and positions himself for the ball to carom off the brick wall. The ball hits the wall and—wait a minute—the ball doesn't come out of the ivy. Sosa goes to the wall and furiously tries to find the ball. It's lost. The third base coach is waving the runner around third. Sosa still can't find the ball. It's going to be an inside-the-park home run. Sosa can only shake his head.

Getting a home run on a lost ball doesn't seem fair. But there are no arguments from the Cubs manager. The "ground rule" at Wrigley Field is that the ivy is in play.

Before every game the managers and umpires meet at home plate to discuss the ground rules. Those are the rules peculiar to the ballpark you're playing in that day. Since everyone knows at the start of the game what is going to happen if the ball goes into the ivy, there are no conflicts to manage when it actually does.

This sports analogy makes a powerful point. When people discuss the ground rules before the game there are fewer arguments and there's considerably less conflict.

When you book an appointment, the prospect is silently wondering . . .

How long is this going to take?
What is going to happen?
Why should I trust you?
When is the close coming?

The best advice I can give you is to cover those questions early in the first face-to-face meeting you have with the prospect. And consider doing it even after the prospect becomes a customer. After watching the movie *Tin Men,* you can see why prospects are suspicious about salespeople and their motives. By discussing your agenda and revealing your process up front, you make a small but very important sale. You sell the prospect on the way you are going to work together.

In Step 10 you gain credibility by revealing your sales process, discussing the ground rules, and framing the issues for the prospect.

Skipping this one step stalls many salespeople in their tracks. Accidental Salespeople feel they are lucky to have an appointment. They skip the vital step of setting the ground rules and selling the prospect on the way they work. When you sell on purpose, you explain your process before you explain your product.

For three years I was the marketing director of a major Wisconsin-based retailer. Part of my job was buying advertising for the company, and for the first six months I kept count in a log. One hundred sixty-eight salespeople called on me in those first six months. Twenty years later I vividly recall that only two of them (Tom Fiewigger and Mark Strachota) approached me professionally. Each came to the meeting with an agenda. They went over the points they wanted to accomplish and told me how long it would take. They always got more of my attention and a larger percentage of my budget than the parade of Accidental Salespeople who passed through my office.

Some of the Accidental Salespeople took a deep breath, sat back in the chair across the desk from me, and settled in like my office was some kind of rest stop. They seemed to be there to gather strength for their next meeting. They certainly weren't prepared for the present one.

"So, Chris, what's going on? Anything coming down for me this week?"

If You Don't Have a Plan Stay in the Car is the title of one of Mark Hanan's many sales books. One of the great things about Hanan's book is that you can benefit from reading the title only. Even if you never cracked the book you would know never to approach a prospect without a premeeting plan.

If you don't have a plan stay in the car—and work on your plan. When you get face-to-face with the prospect, reveal your plan. The first face-to-face meeting is the best time to use the first Magic Phrase, "This is the way I work."

Share with the prospect what you want to accomplish. Tell her how much time you want. Describe the steps you will take to make an intelligent proposal.

Quit hiding your agenda. Get it out in the open early.

Tell the truth. Whatever you do, don't apologize for being there or say, "Thank you for your time." Your time is just as valuable as the prospect's. Avoid trite phrases like, "I'm not here to sell you anything." Because you are.

Accidental Salespeople say those things because they don't know any better. You do. You now use the Magic Phrases to set yourself apart.

"In preparing for the meeting I . . ."

"This is the way I work."

"This is a non-decision-making, fact-finding meeting."

Believe me, buyers can feel the difference when they are approached with purpose. Research from *Purchasing* magazine reveals that lack of preparation and lack of interest or purpose top the list of things buyers dislike about sellers.[1] Salespeople who walk in the door without interest or purpose show very little curiosity about the customer's business. Their purpose (such as it is) for being there is to see what is happening, not to make something happen. "Your account has just been assigned to me," said one salesperson as he walked into my office. "All right," I thought to myself, "another new salesperson to break in." The approach that evidences a complete lack of interest or purpose is, "I was just in the area and

I thought I'd drop by to see if you need anything." You've been warned. By purposefully avoiding the two things buyers dislike the most, you instantly separate yourself from the pack of Accidental Salespeople who just don't get it.

I have always been a "tool maker." I realized a long time ago that speaking or writing about sales is not enough. By including tools that help you put the learning into action, I can get you to DO something instead of just know it.

Education without action is entertainment. To know and not to do is not to know.

Premeeting Planner

The premeeting planner in Figure 8-1 gives you an immediately actionable sales tool. Neil Rackham, author of *SPIN Selling,* differentiates between simple and complex sales.[2] Most of you make complex sales that require multiple meetings and involve long-term commitments and big-ticket products and services. Chances are you will meet with more than one decision maker during the selling process.

You will have to "advance" the prospect through your sales process. You will ask for a lot of things before you ask for the order. Get your prospects used to doing things you ask them to do. Within reason, prospects will do low-risk things for you if there is some benefit in it for them.

Pay close attention to question three, "Have I given or can I give the customer a premeeting assignment. Accidental Salespeople tend to be shy about asking for too much or probing too deeply. When you start selling on purpose, you will ask your prospect to do little things for you. You want to start with easy things for them to say "Yes" to and progress to higher-risk, higher-payoff "asks."

It makes sense. A prepared prospect is a better prospect. But unless you ask prospects to prepare, odds are they won't.

What do we know for sure? Your prospects are busy people. They don't sit around thinking about what you're doing or how the next meeting with you is going to go. Unless you ask them to.

Figure 8-1.   Ladies and gentlemen, I have completed all of my premeeting checks.

Premeeting Planner

Client
Date

One major difference between top performers and moderate performers in any field—and especially in sales—is the way they prepare to do their jobs.

Precall planning is not just thinking about what you will say. It is creating the qualifying questions you will ask and deciding what information you will share.

You're not selling your product or service; you're selling a solution to your prospect's problem. So first you've got to discover a problem you can solve, and to do that you'll need to ask some strategic questions.

Precall planning lets you determine what success means <u>before</u> every call instead of after the call.

How can I manage this sale?

1. At what stage of the process am I with this prospect? (Steps 1 through 16)

2. What new business moves can I make with this prospect today?

3. Have I given or can I give the prospect a premeeting assignment?

4. Have I completed all the steps to this point? Anything need to be firmed up?

5. What can I read, research, or do to have a Level 3 "moment" with this prospect? (Trade press, Web site, etc.)

6. If this meeting is successful, what will happen?

7. What will I ask the prospect to do?

8. What is my fall-back position if the customer says "No" to my first ask?

9. What evidence will I bring to the meeting to support my position?

10. What are the benefits to the prospect for doing what I'm suggesting?

11. What questions will I ask?

12. What information will I share?

13. What preparation will I tell the client about?

14. Should I open the meeting with the words, "In preparing for this meeting, I . . ." ?

15. How can I frame the issues?

16. What do I want to know about the prospect's company?

17. What do I want to learn about the prospect?

18. What information do I want the prospect to know about me? (Self-disclosure)

19. Do I have Level 3 and 4 information to present as well as Level 1 and 2?

An e-mail, fax, or written note that gets them to complete a small task before your next meeting puts you at a subtle advantage. Instead of just confirming your upcoming meeting (always a good idea), consider giving the prospect a specific task to prepare to make the meeting more productive. Here's how a fax or an e-mail might read:

> John,
>   Looking forward to our meeting tomorrow at 9:00. I plan to explore these issues. How do you rate the level of service you are getting from your current supplier? What does "good" look like? What does "excellent" look like from your perspective? In order to save time tomorrow, please take a few minutes to think about that today. Thanks.
>
> Chris

> Mary, See you at 11:00 on Tuesday. In preparing for our meeting, I came across an article that I'd like to discuss. Would you please skim this article and give me your reaction to the highlighted segment when we get together? Chris.

Giving the prospect a premeeting assignment can be as simple as sending over the four or five bullet points of your agenda by e-mail and asking the customer to add his agenda items to it. Even if the prospect doesn't add agenda items, he's read your ideas and thought about the meeting. That's the point.

Control the things you can control before and during an appointment. You can control how much you prepare. You can plan the meeting and set goals for it. You can ask the prospect to prepare to get the most out of the meeting. You can share your agenda with the prospect. All of these little things make a big difference. Admittedly, reading an article is a small, low-risk task to ask of the prospect. Get the prospects used to doing little things you ask. By the time you ask for the order, they will be used to doing what you ask them to do.

Use the Premeeting Planner to note your goals and to preplay the meeting in your head before it happens. See yourself sharing your agenda and information. If this is your first appointment, you may want to "frame the issues" before you move to the Customer Needs Analysis. Here's why.

People have a hard enough time talking to strangers. Think about how hard it is for them to reveal their **problems** to a stranger.

One of my favorite cartoons shows a couple sitting in front of a desk. Seated at the desk is the marriage counselor. The caption reads: "Well, Doc, besides money, in-laws, and sex, we don't really have any serious marital problems."

Therapy is an interesting process. You pay a counselor a hefty fee to listen to your problems and you still may hide the problem from the therapist for months, or even years, until you feel comfortable enough to confront the real issue.

You're not a therapist, and a majority of your prospects don't need therapy. Still, buyers don't reveal real needs and problems to salespeople they have just met and have no reason to trust. Period.

The consultative process has become ingrained in the collective sales consciousness. We have trained salespeople to ask questions first to discover a problem or need. Then, and only then, should you talk about your product, process, or service. The question remains: **Why** should prospects answer your questions and reveal their problems to you? This is the first time they have ever laid eyes on you.

Even if you have never seen *The Music Man,* you must have heard the song "Trouble." "Trouble that starts with a capital T and that rhymes with P and that stands for Pool." Professor Harold Hill gives us a powerful demonstration of how to frame the issues for a prospect before you make your presentation or even before you do a Customer Needs Analysis.

$2 Sales Training Video
The Music Man[3]

Professor Harold Hill is a traveling salesman who goes where the people are as green as the money. On the train, one salesman laments, "I've just been run out of town because of Harold Hill. He goes around selling band instruments . . . and he don't know one note from another. Territory's tough enough without him fouling up the nest. He's a flim-flam man."

Harold Hill arrives in River City, Iowa, as the Fourth of July weekend approaches. There he runs into one of his former shills, Marcellus.

"They got no call for a Boy's Band in this town. Anything these Iowa folks don't already have they do without." Harold Hill is not easily discouraged.

He's looking for a problem, an angle. He needs an opening so he can launch his sales pitch.

"You remember the pitch," says Hill. "What's new around here? If I'm going to get your town out of the serious trouble it's in, I'll need to create a desperate need in your town for a Boy's Band."

Turns out there's a new pool table over at the Pleez-All Billiard Parlor, and that's the only opening Professor Harold Hill needs.

"Either you are closing your eyes to a situation you do not wish to acknowledge. Or you are not aware of the caliber of disaster indicated by the presence of a pool table in your community. Well, you've got trouble my friend. . . ."

After getting the townsfolk worried about the deleterious effect a pool table might have, Hill paints a picture of a parade led by town kids playing seventy-six trombones.

He builds alliances, gets the city council on his side, and ultimately sells his band instruments by the Wells Fargo wagon load to the townsfolk.

But then, instead of leaving town, he falls in love with Marian, the librarian, and decides to stay.

The Music Man details the power of framing the issues for an entire town. Instead of starting with his product, Hill starts with the implications of having a pool table in River City. So that's lesson 1: *Frame the issue.*

There are two other lessons I missed the first ten times I watched this $2 Sales Training Video.

2. Don't be afraid of a tough territory. The other salespeople stayed on the train rather than tried to sell to Iowans. Harold Hill saw Iowa as a personal challenge to his sales skills. He went there "on purpose." As a result, he had no competition.

3. Sell concepts instead of products. It's true that Harold Hill did not always use the most ethical sales tactics. But if you simply dismiss him as a con man, you miss one of the most valuable lessons from the film: He was selling a concept. Hill understood that he was not selling trombones and trumpets. He had a much more important concept. He sold "a way to keep our children moral after school." Once the River City citizens bought that concept, they couldn't part with their money fast enough.

Peter Drucker (there is only one Higher Authority) tells us, "The customer rarely buys what the business thinks it's selling. Top performers in every industry sell concepts. That is why they are top performers."

Harold Hill was a pitchman. Today's sales techniques have evolved from pitching to consulting. At the same time, we've left behind some of the good things the pitchman brought to the table—things like passion and painting vivid pictures of a better way of life. Harold Hill is a spellbinder. He's his own visual aid. He creates a vision of a River City Boy's Band and gets the townsfolk to imagine a better way of life.

Pitching product is different than finding real needs and filling them. On the other hand, being able to find a problem and create urgency has become almost a lost art. Accidental Salespeople go into a prospect's office to see what's happening. Harold Hill went into River City to **make** something happen. Watch the film from that perspective and you'll absorb valuable sales lessons.

Trouble Talk

Successful salespeople use stories, metaphors, and analogies instead of catalogs, spec sheets, and price lists. They paint vivid pictures of a better way of living or doing business. They get people to imagine the enjoyment of a better life before they actually have it.

During the first appointment, you want prospects to feel at ease with you. You also want them to become somewhat ill at ease with the status quo. You want to frame some issues and point out the "Trouble" they may be in if they don't take action.

In order to frame the issues for a prospect, you need an all-purpose "Trouble Talk." This Trouble Talk, or credibility presentation, should focus on real problems that people face if they don't implement your solution.

As a speaker and trainer on sales, when I meet with a prospect for the first time, I'll often send The Chart ahead and I always have a copy with me. My Trouble Talk goes something like this.

> My experience is that most people get into sales accidentally. They don't want to be seen as pushy salespeople. After all, the only salespeople portrayed in the media are high-pressure types with low self-esteem. That's not how they want to be seen, so they default to Level 1. They don't understand that the opposite of pushy is professionally persistent. Does that make sense? Our programs and processes help teach your Accidental Salespeople how to sell on purpose. We set their preference at Level 2 and show them how to have conscious Level 3 and 4 "moments." That helps them leverage their results at every stage of your selling process.

When I move into the consultation phase, I'll ask the prospect how many members of his team are operating at Level 1. Now he's using my model to answer questions about his problems.

"Can you see that some of your salespeople are operating at Level 1?"

"Chris, I have four Level 1 people on my team and one of them is our top producer."

By framing the issues and using my model to discuss the prospect's problem, I have established more trust and credibility. I'm tempted to say, "Well, you've got trouble, my friend." Sharing information is not the same as presenting your solution.

Do you have a Trouble Talk? Can you frame the issues for a buyer? There is a lot to be said for listening to the prospect. Still, there also is something to be said for having something to **say** to the prospect to build credibility and trust. When the prospect sees you as a person who knows what you're doing, he or she will reveal more to you.

Complete these sentences and you are on your way to having a Trouble Talk of your own. After you deliver your Trouble Talk, you will have a prospect who is more willing to go through your process.

Trouble Talk Template

One of the problems that cost businesses a lot of (money, time, hassles) is . . .

According to research by _____, this problem is . . .

(Tell a story.) One of our customers documented a savings of _____ by . . .

My observations/experiences have been . . .

Moreover, research indicates that . . .

It is especially costly in terms of lost . . .

Unchecked, it leads to . . .

But it doesn't have to be that way. Hundreds (thousands) of customers are benefiting from _____ because . . .

Our research into the problem has caused us to approach the problem from . . .

Would you be willing to explore how _____ could help you improve your . . . ?

You now have the basis for a Trouble Talk of your own. You tell the stories and paint pictures of happy customers enjoying the benefits of using your product. You help them visualize the problems they will continue to deal with if they don't use your product. When the prospect sees he is not alone in his distress, and that you have helped others in his situation, you are more likely to have a more productive, fact-finding session. To see how framing the issues can work in real life, consider . . .

Accidental Sales Training Seminar
The Black Pants

My wife, Sarah, is picking me up at O'Hare airport and we are spending our anniversary weekend in Chicago. The plan is to have dinners at two new restaurants and enjoy a nonwork weekend together in a nice hotel.

"I don't want you to wear one of the blue suits that you always speak in, so I packed the new linen jacket I got you for Christmas and some slacks," my wife tells me. As I unpack I discover that the slacks are the ones I've outgrown. They fit when I bought them, but today they are a little snug in the waist.

I could get them on, but I couldn't sit down. So it is a problem. "Of all the black slacks that are hanging in my closet, why did you pack these?" I ask.

"Because they were in your closet. Why were they in the closet if they don't fit?"

"I'll lose the weight some day. Tell you what, I'll just wear this suit to dinner."

"Oh no, you won't. I visualized this dinner and you're wearing the jacket. We're going to go shopping and get you a new pair of black pants."

Our hotel is on Michigan Avenue and out the door is one store after another. The first four do not have a pair of black slacks in my size. It is now about 6:45 P.M. We walk into Lord and Taylor in Water Tower Place.

The salesperson approaches and I pretty much tell him the story you've been reading. I say, "I need a pair of black pants, 38 waist, 34 inseam. They should cost no more than $40."

The salesperson doesn't flinch. He goes off and looks through the racks of slacks. When he comes back he says, "Sir, I couldn't find anything in your size in that price range." (Note that he could just as easily have said, "We don't have anything that cheap in the store.")

"May I show you what I found?"

"You may show me, but I want a $40 pair of pants."

With great flourish he drapes the legs of the pants over one arm and presents them almost as though they were a bottle of fine wine at the restaurant I am trying to get to.

"Do you know the Burberry brand, sir?"

"Listen, I've got **suits** that cost less than that pair of Burberry pants. I just want a nice pair of $40 precut pants today."

"Sir, do you ever wear braces?" he says, ignoring my whining.

"Occasionally."

"Good, because these have the braces buttons already sewn in. They have an interior lining to the knee so that they will hold the crease longer and require less dry cleaning and pressing. That will save you money in the long run."

"Okay, how much?"

"Sir, they are only $120."

"Look, I appreciate the quality, but I have several pairs of black pants hanging in my closet at home. I just want some $40 pants."

"I understand. Shall we make this your backup pair?"

Now I'd never heard of a "backup pair" of pants. "What do you mean?"

"Well, it means that you can shop for a while

longer, and if you can't find another pair of pants, these will be here for you."

"This is my backup pair, then," I agree.

As I turn to walk to yet another store, he asks another question.

"By the way, what time is your function?"

"Our reservation is for eight o'clock." By this time I have only seventy-five minutes until dinner.

"The reason I ask is that these pants have to be tailored. Where are you staying?"

"Just down the street at the Hyatt."

"Good. If I can get the tailor to work on them, you could get back here fairly quickly."

(Now I'm mentally down another twenty minutes.)

"How far is it from your hotel to the restaurant?" Sarah points out that it's a good fifteen minutes.

"Before you go, just let me make sure I can get them tailored fast enough if you do decide to buy."

He picks up a phone and starts an animated discussion with a person, to this day, I believe is the tailor.

"No, tonight. . . . Uh-hum. . . . It's his anniversary. Can you do it?"

Now he's selling the tailor on going to work for me, putting my project at the top of a huge list of alterations.

"I'll ask," he says into the telephone. Then, turning to me, "Straight legs or cuffs, sir?"

"Straight legs are fine," I say, knowing that I have just invested in a pair of Burberry pants.

"I'll run them right down to the tailor. Will that be Lord and Taylor charge or some other method of payment?"

He sold me a pair of pants for $120. The sales seminar he put on was free, a value-added clinic on keeping the customer focused on the problem. He kept framing the issues for me. All of a sudden, he was selling the concept of getting to my function and looking good instead of justifying the price.

My anniversary dinner was saved and although I've

thrown out a lot of other mementos, the black pants still hang in my closet.

Accidental Salesperson Axiom:
When you control the focus of the meeting,
you control the meeting.

Corollary:
Keeping the focus on the prospect's problem
helps you sell faster.

The salesperson framed the issues for me. I could keep looking or I could take action. He let me know what would happen if I kept looking. He kept me focused on my date, my dinner reservation, my travel time.

He also did a brilliant job of asking questions and keeping the sale open long enough to get it closed, which we will deal with when we talk about qualifying the prospect in the next chapter.

Notes

1. James P. Morgan. "Are Your Suppliers' Sales Reps Ready to Go to Bat for You?" *Purchasing,* June 3, 1993.
2. Neil Rackham. *SPIN Selling* (New York: McGraw-Hill, 1988).
3. *The Music Man.* 1962. Directed by Morton DaCosta. 176 minutes. Warner Bros. Videocassette.

Chapter 9

Do You Qualify?

Steps 12 (Continued) and 13

The pants salesperson kept asking questions until I realized I had to buy the Burberry pants right then and there. To shop any longer would have meant being late to dinner and even losing our reservation. He sold me a $120 pair of pants and I got a free seminar on qualifying.

Buyers really do like good salespeople. They want to be given compelling reasons to act. They want to feel certain the purchase they have made is the right one.

Buyers also get frustrated when you don't sell them correctly. Some go elsewhere. At least one buyer put her frustration in writing and faxed it to her vendors. This memo is so powerful, I've labeled it . . . The Prospect's Plea.

Accidental Sales Training Seminar
The Prospect's Plea

To: All Sales Representatives
From: Ellen Armstrong
Subject: Conditions for Seeing Me

You have requested some of my valuable time. I understand that it is your job to do this. You must understand that if I saw every representative who requested an appointment, it

would be a full-time job. I may agree to see you if you ad-
here to the following guidelines.

- Do not attempt to sell me anything until you understand
  my needs, challenges, and past experiences.
- Do not pressure me into doing business with you. The
  more you **push**, the less I will respond.
- Don't demean and criticize your competitors. If you do
  this, I will ask you to leave. I don't mind if you make valid
  comparisons. Gossip, however, contributes nothing of
  value to my business.
- Be clear, concise, and articulate. If I agree to see you, I
  expect you to describe with the highest degree of professionalism how your product will benefit my business. If
  you ramble, you will lose my attention.
- I prefer ideas rather than programs. Be prepared to offer
  me your best ideas and opportunities. Programs that give
  me a "good deal" on products that don't best fit my
  needs tend to work better for you than for me. Show me
  plans that you would buy if you were me.
- Be a resource. Learn about my business and show me that
  you care. You can't get results for me if you don't know
  what's going on in my world.
- Listen as much as you talk, and don't waste my time.

Now you have my conditions for an appointment. Please
sign it and mail it back to me. Then, call again and I will
consider giving you my valuable time.

That's what I've been trying to tell you for this entire
book, and this disgruntled buyer goes and does it in one
memo. Her memo is a plea to her vendors to take their selling
efforts to the next level. She doesn't have The Chart or use
the term Level 1, but she clearly is fed up with the number of
Level 1 salespeople she is seeing and the quality of the meetings they are having. She clearly describes the Level 2 behavior she prefers, and even suggests that people have Level 3
"moments" with her ("Be a resource").

Figure 9-1.   You are tracking the steps you've taken and the time elapsed between steps.

Ten Most Wanted List

The 16-Step Selling Process Box Score

Based on your own selling cycle, set a time frame to accomplish all 16 steps.

1. Identify businesses (prospects/clients)
2. Identify decision maker

Column headers (angled):
3. Seed (describe)
4. Seed (describe)
5. Letter
6. Dial
7. Contact decision maker
8. Book first appointment
9. Confirm the first appointment
10. Complete 1st app't. Sell your process & frame the issue
11. Book Customer Needs Analysis
12. Complete Customer Needs Analysis
13. Book the proposal
14. Write the proposal
15. Make the proposal
16. Confirm the order (close)

	3	4	5	6	7	8	9	10	11	12	13	14	15	16
Design Concepts Julian Albrecht (6/12) 414-221-2623	6/12 G.M. mag art.	6/15 WSJ art.	6/18	6/21 6/24	6/24	6/24 for 6/28	6/24	6/28						
Totals														

Decision makers ID'd ÷ total prospects		Contacts ÷ dials	App'ts confirmed ÷ app'ts booked	CNA booked ÷ 1st app't completed	Proposals booked ÷ CNAs	Proposals made ÷ prop's written	Sales closed ÷ prospects started
% Decision makers ID'd		% Reached	% App'ts conf'd	% CNAs booked	% Prop's booked	% Prop's made	Gross Closing Ratio
	Dials ÷ decision makers ID'd	App'ts booked ÷ contacts	1st app't completed ÷ app'ts confirmed	CNAs completed ÷ CNAs booked	Prop's written ÷ prop's booked	Sales closed ÷ prop's made
	% Decision makers dialed	% App'ts booked	% App'ts completed	% CNAs completed	% Prop's written	% Closed

You have completed the first meeting with your prospect. You have framed the issues and given your Trouble Talk. You have impressed the prospect, piqued his interest, and established credibility. You either book the Customer Needs Analysis meeting (Step 11) at that point or you move ahead to that stage in the current meeting.

In either case, be clear with yourself and with your prospect that this is what is happening. Say, "We're moving to the data-gathering stage of your sales process."

Here is the critical step every Accidental Salesperson skips: Before you start firing questions at the prospect, take time to sell the prospect on the benefits of answering the questions and going through your consultative process.

Consultative selling is the norm today. Every book you read and seminar you attend advises you to ask questions in order to determine needs. It is obvious that not everyone practices this kind of selling, however. Neil Rackham's *SPIN Selling* is the breakthrough book that documented Rackham's research into what top sales performers do differently than moderate performers. His conclusion is that top performers ask better questions.

There is no doubt that asking questions will help you. You'll gain valuable information with which to sell more of your product.

But how will answering your questions benefit the prospect? Answer that before you start asking questions, and the quality of the answers you get will be much better.

You've done everything right up to this point. You have described your process to the prospect. He has bought the way you sell. You are very close to being in position to propose what you sell, but you need to know more.

Lay out both your rationale and the benefits of asking the questions to the prospect. Way back in Chapter 2, I told the story about the car dealer who canceled his advertising. He demanded to meet with all of the media representatives for twenty minutes each in one day. He told me that it was the most boring day of his life. When I presented the benefit of getting an intelligent proposal, he was more than happy to invest an hour and a half with me instead of twenty minutes. An intelligent proposal may or may not be a strong enough benefit for your prospect, but it's a start.

On the other hand, you may want to whip out a copy of The Chart and do a little self-disclosure:

"I got into sales accidentally, but I sell on purpose. I want to create customers instead of make sales. By going through this process and answering my questions, you'll gain some new insights because I'll ask some questions for free that you'd pay a consultant to ask you. I'll be in a position to customize a solution instead of having to guess at what you might need. Fair enough?"

Don't try to hide what's happening and slide into your consultation. If you want the prospect to disclose more information, you have to disclose some information too.

Making that one refinement will differentiate you and put one more point in your credibility column.

Your company may have a questionnaire for you to fill out. You may need technical information in order to engineer a solution. So in this chapter I'm simply going to give you a wonderfully simple, all-purpose Customer Needs Analysis approach that will enhance whatever you are doing now. I learned about it in . . .

Accidental Sales Training Seminar
The MCI Salesperson

I'm a sales trainer, but I'm also a buyer. I had agreed to sit down with Jeff, a salesperson from MCI (now part of MCI WorldCom). He was in our conference room to find out if he could get our telephone business. I wasn't impressed with his opening.

"You have a beautiful office." said Jeff.

"Jeff, you know I'm a sales trainer. Don't do the beautiful office opening."

"Seriously, we're a multibillion dollar company and your office is nicer than our Madison office. Just an observation."

"Thanks." Then he impressed me.

"Chris, we want to do more than sell cheap long-distance rates. We want to offer communication solutions. In order for me to see the business from your perspective, I'd like to do a quick Force-Field Analysis.

(Good job of explaining why he was doing a Force-Field Analysis, I observed, but what, I wondered, is a Force-Field Analysis?)

Jeff took a legal pad and drew a line at the bottom. "Let's go back to Day 1." He wrote Day 1 next to the line. "Day 1 was when?"

"Well, Sarah and I founded this company in January of 1983."

"Okay." He continued talking as he drew another line above the bottom line and wrote "Today" next to it. "From 1983 until today, you have done a lot of things to get you to this level of success." As Jeff said that, he drew four arrows from the Day 1 line pointing upward to the Today line.

All I can tell you is that each one of those arrows elicited a response from me. With no further questions, I was labeling the arrows and Jeff took notes. Those arrows made me talk and I gave him very specific information about our philosophy, our business practices, and our strengths as a company.

When I'd labeled all the arrows and was starting to run out of steam, he took the piece of paper and added a line at the top. "Let's call this line, 'the next level.' It's the next level of growth or the dream you have for improving your business. What is keeping you from getting there?"

With that, he drew four arrows from the top line to the Today line. It was obvious that these were the forces holding us back, and I ranted for ten minutes about my competition, the cost of marketing, and several other problems.

He gained some valuable insights into our business, and I experienced a new kind of consultation that worked so well I immediately started teaching it in my seminars. There must be some sales trainer reading this book who will claim that I stole it from him or her. But I've never read about this technique, I've never seen a seminar on it. I experienced it in another Accidental Sales Seminar.

The Force-Field Analysis doesn't really require a form. It works better when you draw it on a white board, legal pad, or placemat at a restaurant. One salesperson told us about doing a Force-Field Analysis on the back of a golf scorecard while he and the prospect were playing a round of golf. Play around with this the next time you need to gain more information.

The Force-Field Analysis works very well when you are presenting it to a committee. You will get many different opinions about what the arrows mean, and you can factor that into your proposal to the committee.

Once your prospect has labeled the arrows, you ask more specific questions to get at the data you need.

Some salespeople know how to ask questions and some don't. Notice the difference between these two questions, which go after the same data.

Example #1:
   "So, what is your budget?" asks the Accidental Salesperson.
   "That's confidential information," the client replies guardedly.

Example #2:
   "In order for me to make an intelligent proposal, I need to know your budget," says the pro.
   "Oh, of course. It's $123,000," says the cooperative prospect.

In Example #2, the salesperson gives the prospect a benefit (intelligent proposal) for providing the information. Example #2 doesn't even look or sound like a question. It's called an imbedded question. Read it again.

"In order for me to make an intelligent proposal, I need to know your budget."

The question doesn't begin with Who, What, When, Where, Why, or How. It doesn't end with a question mark. The question (What's your budget anyway?) is imbedded in the statement. You may have used imbedded questions accidentally in the past. Use them on purpose and your needs analysis meetings will be discussions instead of interrogations. Here are several examples of imbedded questions.

"I'd be interested in learning about your criteria for making the change."

"I want to understand the decision-making process you are going through."

"Talk about how this might improve your operation."

"Tell me more about the problems you've had in the past with this kind of equipment."

Gathering data and assessing prospects' needs is a process. Too often salespeople go through the motions of filling out the questionnaires so they can go right to their presentation. When you're selling on purpose, your mindset is that every prospect interaction is an opportunity to gain more information and qualify the prospect better. Once the prospect becomes a customer, the data gathering continues. The situation is always changing.

Today your prospects want you to come to the table knowing the answers to the questions they used to have time to sit down and answer. Your prospects are too pressed for time to teach you things you can learn yourself by hitting a Web site.

Accidental Salesperson Axiom:
Asking questions is the answer to most sales problems.

Corollary:
If you listen more than you talk,
you will seem much more intelligent than you really are.

Sales trainers talk about listening until they are blue in the face. Maybe that's the problem: We **talk** about listening. Virtually every salesperson has been told to ask questions and listen more. There is no better way to understand the power of listening than to watch . . .

$2 Sales Training Video
Being There[1]

Chance, the gardener, has lived most of his life inside the Washington, D.C., town house and walled garden of the old man. While the word "retarded" isn't used, Chance cannot take care of himself. Louise, the maid, feeds him. His life is limited to tending the garden and watching television. His existence, and his mind, seem simple indeed.

Then the old man dies. There is no money to take care of Chance and he finds himself on the street. He stops to watch television in the window and see himself on the monitor. As he backs up into the street, a limousine backs into his leg, trapping it between its bumper and a parked car. In the limo, Eve (Shirley MacLaine), fearing a lawsuit and seeing how impeccably dressed Chance is, insists he come home with her to have a doctor look at the leg. (Her husband is very ill and has around-the-clock care.)

Chance is hurt and hungry. Having nowhere else to go, he agrees to go home with Eve.

Eve asks Chance his name. He tells her he is Chance, the gardener. She hears it as "Chauncy Gardener" and proceeds to introduce her friend, Chauncy, to her husband, Ben.

Ben and Eve live in a huge mansion. Aging millionaire Ben still wields power. He is on a first-name basis with the President of the United States, who visits his old friend at the mansion. Ben introduces Chauncy to his friend the President and the fun begins. Chauncy is soon on a first-name basis with the President. When the President asks him what he thinks about the difficult economy, Chauncy talks about the only thing he knows anything about—the garden.

"In the garden there is spring, summer, fall, winter, and then spring again," he tells the President.

When the President looks puzzled, Ben interprets, "What I think our fine young friend is trying to say is that we put up with the seasons in the garden, but not in our economy."

At a party, women find Chance incredibly attractive. He says exactly what is on his mind because he is not clever enough to deceive anyone, and people find his candor refreshing rather than rude. When the Russian ambassador speaks to Chauncy in Russian, he laughs. The ambassador mistakenly believes Chauncy speaks Russian and regales him with his favorite Russian poetry. Chauncy just maintains eye contact and smiles. The ambassador is none the wiser.

The very next day the President quotes his good friend Chauncy Gardner in a nationally televised press conference. Soon Chauncy appears on television, speaking metaphorically about gardening. People attribute much wisdom to the uttering of this simple-minded man. By the end of the film some are touting Chauncy as the next Presidential candidate, even as some other people discover his true identity.

Being There demonstrates the power of saying little and listening a lot. Sure it's a satire on politics and power, but Jerzy Kosinski accidentally created a compelling sales-training film. Observe how Chance, played by Peter Sellers, gets his power. Chauncy kept conversations going with eye contact and an occasional question. When he said nothing, people just kept talking. When he looked at them, they told him more. When he finally spoke, people listened and then attributed great wisdom to his every utterance.

Don't be afraid of dead air. Your silence may be powerful.

The other powerful lesson is the importance of clothing. Chance, the gardener, was the same size as the old man, who dressed impeccably. Wearing the old man's clothes, Chance made a powerful first impression with his clothes, if not with his wit. People assumed that he was a person of importance and treated him accordingly.

When you are curious and interested, you'll find that you get stories from the prospect and not just dry facts. When prospects tell you their stories and engage you, they become emotionally involved in the process. They go beyond the facts and give you more inside, behind-the-scenes information. Instead of moving quickly through your list of questions, take the time to ask follow-up questions and get the stories behind the facts.

You must really want to know the answers to the questions you are asking. Chance listened because he didn't really want to talk. Too many salespeople simply feign listening while waiting until it's their turn to talk.

Every time you meet with the prospect, you have an opportunity to update your database and discover more problems you can help solve. Qualifying is part of Step 12 in your sales process. You need to ask more questions in order to make an intelligent first presentation.

Old-school sales trainers harangued their audiences with the acronym A-B-C. "Always Be Closing," they said. In today's sales environment, it might be more appropriate to leave you with a new acronym: N-Q-Q. Never Quit Qualifying.

Once you have qualified the prospect and have determined there is a problem you can solve, book the meeting for the proposal. Don't leave the needs analysis meeting without an appointment.

One of the biggest mistakes Accidental Salespeople make is waiting until they have the proposal written before they book the appointment to present it. If you book the proposal appointment (Step 13), you can't procrastinate. You have a compelling deadline that propels your proposal writing.

(With the Proposal-Writing Template in the next chapter, you'll easily meet that deadline.)

Depending on how long and involved your proposals are, you may want to limit the number of needs analysis interviews. For example, if you have done two needs analysis interviews, don't do another one until you have converted one of the interviews into a proposal. Then allow yourself one more interview. Proposal meetings are where you make your money. You may love having dozens of interested prospects. But until you make a proposal and ask prospects to invest real money, you'll never know how interested they really are.

Note

1. *Being There.* Directed by Hal Ashby. 79 minutes. Lorimar Film Entertainment. Videocassette.

Chapter 10

Doing the Work before You Get Paid for It and Other Secrets of Success

Steps 14 and 15

It's time to take the mystery and misery out of proposal writing. Using the Proposal-Writing Template as your guide, you will soon be including Level 2, 3, and 4 pages in your proposals. This one refinement automatically makes every proposal you write and present more prospect focused. You'll learn how to plug into a powerful formula found in an obvious, but overlooked sales-training video. By the end of this chapter you will be turning out proposals that impress your prospects and increase your sales.

There is an interesting story behind the Proposal-Writing Template. A major Canadian broadcaster had retained me to do some management training. The goal was to create nationwide standards of performance for various sales teams. The company wanted to be able to judge a salesperson in Moose Jaw, Saskatchewan, by the same standards as a salesperson in Toronto. The broadcasting company was looking for objective ways to measure what "good" looked like in the organization in order to train everyone to that standard.

A standard is a measurable indicator of performance, often involving a consequence. In the past, most standards for salespeople involved quantity instead of quality. The Chart changes some of that. You still have to make a certain number of proposals, but making five Level 2 proposals may result in more sales than making ten Level 1 proposals. That is so obvious that even old school sales managers buy the logic of it.

The problem has been **measuring** the quality of a proposal before you present it. The Proposal-Writing Template solves that problem.

In preparing for the management training session, I requested and received copies of real proposals the company's salespeople had already made. Unfortunately, by the time the proposals stopped arriving at our offices, I had more than a thousand pages of reading to do to prepare for the upcoming manager's meeting. I actually lugged these proposals from city to city as I conducted other seminars. But at the end of the each day, I felt too tired to attack the intimidating stack of papers. Even though the weight of those papers in my suitcase was nearly enough to pull my shoulder from its socket, the proposals remained unread until the day before the management training seminar. However, in this case, procrastination proved to be a good thing.

On my way to Winnipeg, where the management meeting was being held, I had a three-hour layover at O'Hare airport and headed for the Red Carpet Club. After settling in I read three appalling proposals in quick succession. There were about eighty more to look at. After skimming the next half dozen, I quit reading. *Why should I be reading these?* I thought. *The managers ought to be experiencing these boring, company-focused proposals the same way I am. They should experience how bad these really are.* I couldn't just tell them. I wanted to let them discover and actually articulate how bad they were. So I designed an exercise.

In Winnipeg, I passed out copies of The Chart to each sales manager. They found it easy enough to talk about the Levels at which different salespeople on their teams were operating.

Then I suggested that if salespeople can have measurable Level 1, 2, 3, and 4 "moments" with their prospects, it might also be possible to measure Level 1, 2, 3, and 4 pages in their proposals. For example, a page about a prospect's problem would be Level 2. A printout of various rates or specs about the product the salespeople were trying to sell would be Level 1, and so on. I had them use The Chart to grade each page of the proposal: 1, 2, 3, or 4. They added the scores and divided that score by the number of pages in the proposal.

Working in pairs, the managers graded proposals their team members had turned out, as well as proposals their partner's team members had written. There were audible groans as they read and graded. The mood in the room was somber.

"My people are cranking out crap, eh?" said one of the managers. "And they're taking the trouble to put a color cover page on it and bind it before they give it to a prospect."

"There was nothing in here about the client," observed another. "It was a pure Level 1 proposal from a person who I thought was operating at a much higher level."

Their people were not trying to turn out bad presentations. They just didn't have a model for what "good" looked like, so they had "defaulted" to Level 1.

There are days when I learn as much from the audience as they learn from me. By the end of this management training seminar, we had made a major breakthrough: There are no pure Level 4 salespeople and there can never be a pure Level 4 proposal. Level 2 became the standard of what "good" looks like in the company. Level 2 proposals were 100 percent better than the Level 1 proposals they were turning out.

The story doesn't end there. For the next three years we worked with this client and others to set down the criteria to measure the different types of pages we found in proposals. The Proposal-Writing Template is the result.

Proposal-Writing Template

You can use the template in Figure 10-1 to check the quality of your proposal before you present it. Use specific sugges-

Figure 10-1. Add quality to every proposal, including Level 2, Level 3, and Level 4 pages in addition to your Level 1 material.

Proposal-Writing Template

Level 1 Pages
❏ Spec sheets
❏ Price lists
❏ Catalog
❏ Brochure
❏ One-sheeters about products
❏ Company press release
❏ Pictures of your plant or operation

Level 2 Pages
❏ A cover page that offers a solution to a problem
❏ A business balance sheet
❏ A problem description page
❏ A problem solution page that shows how your product or service addresses the prospect's need
❏ Testimonial letters from your satisfied customers

	Level 1 Account Executive	Level 2 Salesperson or Problem Solver	Level 3 Professional Salesperson	Level 4 Sales and Marketing Professional
Level of trust	Neutral or distrustful	Some credibility	Credible to highly credible; based on salesperson's history	Complete trust based on established relationships and past performance
Goal/call objective	To open doors; to "see what's going on"	To persuade and make a sale or to advance the prospect through the process	Customer creation and retention; to "find the fit"; to upgrade the client and gain more information	To continue upgrading and increase share of business
Approach and involvement	Minimal or nonexistent	Well-planned; work to get prospect to buy into the process	True source of industry information and "business intelligence"	Less formal and more comfortable because of trust and history
Concern or self-esteem issue	Being liked	Being of service, solving a problem	Being a resource	Being an "outside insider"
Precall preparation	Memorize a canned pitch or "wing it"	Set call objectives; prescript questions; articulate purpose–process payoff	Research trade magazines, Internet; analyze client's competition	Thorough preparation, sometimes with proprietary information unavailable to other reps
Presentation	Product literature, spec sheets, rate sheets	Product solution for problem they uncover during needs analysis	Systems solutions	Return on investment proof and profit improvement strategies
Point of contact	Buyer or purchasing agent	End users as well as buyer or purchasing agent	Buyers, end users, and an "internal coach" or advocate within client's company	"Networked" through the company; may be doing business in multiple divisions

DEFAULT ▲ PREFERENCE SETTINGS

Level 3 Pages
❏ Facts from the client's annual report or Web site
❏ Facts from industry trade publications
❏ Facts from Internet searches
❏ Facts from business publications
❏ Quotes from business experts
❏ Information on the client's competition that relates to your recommendation
❏ Industry research

Level 4 Pages
❏ Research on the client's customer
❏ Focus group information
❏ Consumer research
❏ Recommendations that affect cost savings, efficiency, and profit enhancements

Lead with Level 3 and 4 pages.

Calculate your score according to this formula: Total points scored on all pages (   ) divided by number of pages in proposal (   ) equals average score of proposal (   ).

tions for Level 3 and 4 pages by going through the checklists. The idea is not to make a thirty-page proposal but to make sure that your five-page proposal has higher-level pages before the unavoidable Level 1 material. I say "unavoidable" because you **have** to discuss price and product specifications. These should follow higher-level pages, however, and not lead off your proposal.

Until you've established that the prospect has a problem and offered proof that your product is the solution, the price and specifications aren't really relevant.

The best thing you can do right now is stop reading this book and grade some of the proposals you have written to see exactly what level you've attained and to set a goal for taking your next proposal to a higher level. Be brutally honest with yourself. If it's a close call, grade yourself on the low side.

Look at all the Level 1 possibilities:

Spec sheets
Price lists
Catalog
Brochure
One-sheet product literature
Company press releases
Pictures of your plant or facility

These are the things Accidental Salespeople automatically reach for as "filler" to bulk up their proposals. They mistakenly believe that their expensive brochures and reams of product literature are important sales tools. After all, their companies have shelving units straining beneath the weight of all the expensive four-color printing. Let's get these pictures of our product into the hands of our prospects, thinks the Accidental Salesperson.

In reality, these Level 1 pages drag down proposal quality. They make a proposal more about the product than about the prospect's problem.

The Proposal-Writing Template prompts you to consider a variety of higher level pages. If I hit my prospect's Web site and find the mission includes training and developing people, you can bet it will appear in one of the first two pages of my proposal. Starting with a Level 3 page that positions my services as a natural extension of the mission adds power.

The Proposal-Writing Template makes great proposals almost as easy to produce as poor ones. You'll soon discover that it's easier to close prospects on higher-level proposals too.

Some salespeople resist written proposals. One seminar participant put it this way: "Chris, what if I go to all this work and the prospect doesn't buy? I will have put in a lot of hours for nothing."

Obviously, you only do proposals for qualified prospects. Still, there will always be a certain amount of uncertainty in selling. One sure thing: To be successful, you are going to have do a lot of work up front for free, hoping that the prospect will pay you later.

Accidental Salesperson Axiom:
Doing the work before you get paid for it is part
of the price of success.

Corollary:
You may put in an honest day's work
and not get an honest day's pay.

If you work on straight commission, you prospect for free. You do a Customer Needs Analysis for free. You do the research and write the proposal for free. Then you **make** the proposal for free. Even when your company pays you a salary or a draw, the client pays you only after you've made a good proposal.

That's the way it works.

At least you don't have to pay to make your presentation to the prospect.

What if you did have to pay to make your presentation? Think about that for a moment. You obviously would put more time and thought into it. You probably would even rehearse it a few times. You would make certain your proposal flowed logically from your opening statement (or question) to the close. You'd make sure you proved each point you made. You'd demonstrate your product's superiority and offer testimonials. You would definitely ask for the order and you would not take the prospect's first "No" for an answer. You would review your key points and ask again, and make certain to combine logical arguments with emotional reasons to get the prospect to act **now** instead of later. Wouldn't you?

That's why our next Sales Training Video is an "infomercial." The producers of these long-form advertisements (infomercials) pay hundreds of thousands of dollars to create and present their sales messages. They cannot afford to leave anything out or anything to chance. The next time you look at *TV Guide,* find a channel that offers paid programming. Tune in for half an hour. (Don't write down the toll-free number.) Take notes on how the advertiser puts together the sales presentation. Then, go and do likewise.

One morning I sat down and watched one infomercial after another and took notes for you. Of course, I now could be making millions buying real estate with no money down. I could have reshaped my body with TaeBo. But, no. I haven't even applied the revolutionary protectant to preserve the paint on my car. I'm still here, trying to help you put together more powerful presentations. Watch and learn.

Free Sales Training Video
Any Infomercial on Television

Every infomercial follows this basic three-step formula:

1. Set forth the problem.
2. Explain the solution.
3. Demonstrate how your product or service best provides the solution.

Infomercial pioneer Alvin Eicoff described the process in his book, *Successful Broadcast Advertising.* In *The Music*

Man, Professor Harold Hill used the same formula to sell band instruments in River City.

Every infomercial begins with a Level 2 "moment." The headline speaks directly to the audience about their problems—not the product. An infomercial for a course on buying real estate with no money down opens with a real person talking about retirement. He says, "For most people when they retire, their home is their saving grace. They sell their big home and buy a smaller one. They invest the difference and live off it. But what if they had five homes?"

The product is the solution to the problem being presented. But you still don't see the real estate course itself. First you see real people who already have benefited from the course. In these testimonials, people talk about other programs they have tried and why this course was the answer to their prayers.

When the infomercial sells an exercise program, people talk about other programs they have tried and why this one is better. Ultimately the inventor of the product or developer of the program comes on and tells the story of how he discovered an amazing secret and how thrilled he is that he can make the world a better place. The storytelling adds credibility and makes the audience feel connected to the people behind the product.

The advertiser explains the solution and then demonstrates exactly how the product provides the solution. The demonstrations in infomercials offer evidence. Richard Simmons uses "before" pictures of very heavy people and then brings the transformed person up on stage. (Tell me you've never cried during a Richard Simmons infomercial.) In an infomercial for a product called Prolong, a spokesperson sprays red lacquer paint on a collector's yellow classic car. The car's owner waits in suspense as the spokesperson easily wipes off the dried lacquer.

All that's left is to ask for the order. "Get out your pen," commands the announcer, "here comes that toll-free number." The announcer summarizes the problem, explains the solution, reminds you of the amazing demonstrations you've just seen, presents the product and the pricing options, and asks you to act now.

Not everyone does. But enough people do. Long-form advertisements sell $75 billion worth of goods and services each year.

"But wait, there's still more."

There always is in infomercials. Most infomercials raise objections that the prospect may be having and answer them before the prospect asks. This is a powerful technique. If you raise the objection first, the prospect is less likely to use it later.

Infomercials also make it clear that the buyer won't be alone. Thousands (even millions) of people have already turned their lives around with this product.

Infomercials compare the price of the product to something completely different. "This course costs less than dinner for two at a nice restaurant." This gets people to think about things they have already purchased instead of comparing the product with a competing product.

Infomercials always make the product part of a "complete system" by adding a booklet, an extra video, or a bottle of some other kind of cleaner or solvent. There is nothing left to buy. You get the complete system for two easy payments.

And finally, there is always a money-back guarantee if the customer is not completely satisfied. This is called risk reversal. It makes it easier for the prospect to give the product a try. You may not be able to offer a money-back guarantee, but the more you can do to assure the prospect there is very little risk, the easier it will be to make the sale.

People who produce and place infomercials pay for the privilege of presenting. They are giving you a free seminar on how to sell. Ignore the lessons at your own risk.

Combining the three-part formula for writing an infomercial and the components suggested in the Proposal-Writing Template provides plenty of structure. You'll find that you start gathering data immediately to fit your proposal-writing format.

One thing I urge you to start doing right away is to put the problem on the cover page. Examples:

How to Eliminate 7 Hours of Costly Downtime per Month
or
How to Transform Your Sales Department
into a Sales Force

It is tempting—but completely unnecessary—to put your company's logo and your name on the cover page. Set forth the problem and you start your proposal with a Level 2 page. Then add pages that explain why your solution is best. **Demonstrate** how your product provides the best solution. **Detail** exactly what the prospect gets and when. And ask for the order.

Written proposals can help you sell, but they shouldn't be asked to sell for you. Think visual aid instead of term paper. Your written proposal is just the outline. You provide the details in conversation. There is a terrible tendency today for salespeople to overuse PowerPoint® presentations and similar tools. They make too many slides and then read them to the prospect. Bad move.

Watch out for one other thing. With bound proposals, bored prospects can read ahead to the investment page and start poring over the specifics instead of considering your rationale and weighing your evidence first.

You control the focus of the presentation by controlling how much you give the prospect at the outset of your meeting. Handing the prospect one page of your proposal at a time lets you control the flow of information. And having limited information on visual aids means that the prospect needs you to "fill in the blanks."

Finally, work on your stories. Spreadsheets make it possible to add page after page of mind-numbing figures to your presentation. Stories add emotion and passion to the evidence you present. You need to present logical **and** emotional reasons for the prospect to buy.

All that is left now is asking for the order.

Chapter 11

"Closing" Is a Funny Word for It

Step 16

Most closing problems aren't really closing problems. Too many Accidental Salespeople never get to the point in their sales process where closing is appropriate.

They don't keep their sales **open** long enough to get them closed.

Still, many sales managers fixate on closing to the exclusion of all the other steps in the process that make closing a "natural outcome" of taking prospects through your process.

"Order acquisition" may be a better term than closing. It reflects the reality that confronts today's salespeople. It takes multiple meetings and help from marketing, engineering, finance, and top management to bring in an order today.

It's a fact that you are often an "orchestrator" as much as you are a salesperson. You have to orchestrate meetings among members of your team and get them working on behalf of members of the buyer's team.

Still, the myth persists among sales managers that if they just had a few more "closers," everything would be all right.

"Killer Wanted"

Not long ago I came across that headline in the "Help Wanted" section of a prominent trade magazine. The company that placed the ad was looking for a salesperson who was a "killer."

That's an interesting hiring standard.

The ad didn't specify other criteria like achievement history, written and oral communication skills, integrity, initiative, and empathy.

"Only killers need apply" was the clear message of the ad.

"Why," I wondered, "wasn't the company seeking a professional salesperson with a proven record of sales and customer satisfaction?"

And what if that company's customers got wind of the fact that the company only hired "killers" and the "killer" was coming to call on them? No doubt the manager who submitted the ad only meant "killer" figuratively.

But the choice of the word indicates that the manager hasn't gotten the message that today's superstars are more like farmers than hunters. They cultivate relationships instead of "bag" an order. They view their clients as partners instead of prey.

Life is one big sales seminar. I've learned more about selling and closing sales by selling sales training than I've learned in any book or seminar about selling. Here's why. When you sell sales training, the prospects are not only going through your sales process, they are also evaluating how they are being sold and deciding whether or not they want their salespeople to represent their company the way you're representing yours.

So anyone who agrees to sit down to talk about buying sales training from me gets a free look at what I'm going to teach them. Let me tell you about the day I quit using any close from a book, tape, or seminar.

Accidental Sales Training Seminar
The Stale Close

Early in my career, I was trying to sell a seminar to Charlie Ferguson. He was a general manager who had used other sales trainers and had recently heard of me.

"Chris, I'm interested in bringing you to town. I just have to have the corporate office sign off on it."

That sounded like a buying signal to me. I immediately went for a "trial close" that I had read about and (alas) was teaching in my seminar.

"Well, Charlie," I said (too) smoothly. "If your corporate office approves it, will we be having the seminar in April or would May work better for you?"

"That was a subordinate question, alternate choice close, Chris," said the prospect.

"Yes, it was."

"Well, it didn't work. Good-bye."

Charlie was offended that I would use a technique on him. He wanted a relationship and not just a seminar, and I used a manipulative, old-school closing line.

It took eleven years to gain that trust back and finally do business with Charlie.

Accidental Salesperson Axiom:
You don't have to trick people into doing business with you.

Corollary:
Never use a closing **line** from any book, tape, or seminar.

Professional buyers go to seminars and learn about the "techniques" that salespeople use to manipulate them. The minute you start using techniques, you lose their trust.

Closing is a funny word:

C – L – O – S – I – N – G

Cross out the C and you are left with a new word:

L – O – S – I – N – G

Eighty-six percent of "closing" is "losing."

Accidental Sales **Managers** (sounds like the title of my

next book) set up this win-lose scenario by focusing on closing the sale instead of advancing prospects throughout the process.

"Who are you going to close?" is asked far more often than "Where are you in the process and what is your strategy for the next step?" Accidental Salespeople get beat up in the field and then take more abuse from their managers when they get back to the office. Instead of coaching their people through the process, sales managers add more pressure.

"You didn't close anyone today?"

They run Level 1 sales meetings that focus on the products to sell instead of the prospects' problems and wonder why their salespeople can't seem to close.

The ultimate Level 1 sales meeting is the "Sales Meeting from Hell" that Alec Baldwin's character, Blake, ran in the dark film about selling real estate, *Glengarry Glen Ross*. This movie is so dark that the first time I saw it, I walked out of the theater, back to the box office, and paid for a ticket to a comedy. It's in this book because, if you do the opposite of everything in the film, you will be a better salesperson.

$2 Sales Training Video
Glengarry Glen Ross[1]

"Coffee is for closers," says Blake, as Jack Lemmon's character gets up to get a cup. Blake is the "guy from downtown" who is in the shabby real estate office to "motivate" the salespeople to get out there and sell real estate.

"We're adding a little something to this month's sales contest," says Blake. "As you all know, first prize is a Cadillac Eldorado. Anybody want to see second prize?" He holds up the prize. "Second prize is a set of steak knives. Third prize is you're fired."

Fear is the motivator in *Glengarry Glen Ross*. The new leads that sales manager Kevin Spacey has locked up in his office become the excuse for not performing.

How can anybody be expected to sell with leads as bad as the ones these salespeople have? The salespeople in the shabby office try to sound like something they are not—rich and powerful. They portray themselves to their customers as power-wielding, connected vice presidents.

"I would feel wrong, not sharing this marvelous opportunity with you," Shelly Levine tells a customer on the phone. He interrupts himself, pretending to order his nonexistent assistant, Grace, to rebook his airline ticket so that he can schedule a meeting with the resistant prospect on the other end of the line.

It is hard to imagine anyone needing a sales job so badly that they would keep one like those portrayed in *Glengarry Glen Ross.* Throughout the film, groups of salespeople meet to talk about how bad things are and complain about leads. They are preoccupied with why they can't sell instead of focused on what they can control. The Glengarry leads are what they need. They are looking for the solution from without, instead of from within.

The salespeople in *Glengarry Glen Ross* got beaten up in the office because their managers thought it would toughen them up when they went on a "sit" with prospects and tried to sell them real estate in their living rooms.

The managers motivated salespeople with prizes and fear. They never worked on the most powerful source of motivation: building belief. As a result, the salespeople focused on the prize (or worried about the punishment) instead of the prospect.

If you weren't a closer, you were a loser.

Belief is a powerful motivator.

A *Success* magazine survey of a thousand top sales performers found that more than half had abandoned any kind of closing technique. Some 56 percent of the salespeople said they just looked the client in the eye and said something like, "This is right for you. Let's do it." Then they waited for the customer to sign the order.

In order to use this close effectively, you have to believe what you are offering is right for the prospect and you have to communicate the **feeling**, not just the closing words.

Let's look at how values, attitudes, and behavior at the time of the sale come together. You ask for the business. Depending on how you ask, you get a Yes, a No, or a Maybe.

The core of the closing sphere is values. You have certain core values that were formed and set in place by the time you were eight. You either looked people in the eye, told the truth, honored your parents, loved God, and/or shared your toys, or you didn't. Your early childhood experience shaped your values. Your parents and grandparents, older siblings, early religious training, and very first teachers played the biggest roles in forming your values. Let's assume your values are solid. After all, you aren't selling drugs or smuggling arms.

You've heard of wearing your heart on your sleeve? Well, your attitudes and beliefs are more malleable and more visible than your values. You can wake up in the morning ready to take on the marketplace. By nine o'clock you may have a canceled order or get a call from an unhappy customer. By noon, you are reading the want ads.

Here's why belief and attitude are so important in selling. Imagine that you have just made your presentation. The prospect is nodding his head and making positive comments. The prospect's questions indicate a strong interest in what you are selling. Your senses tell you that now is the time to ask for the order.

All of us have "voices" in our head. If you've ever talked to yourself and answered back, then you know there are at least two people in there. But you hear other voices, some more loudly than others.

The voice of the sales trainer says to you, "Look the man in the eye and say, 'This is right for you, let's do it.'"

The voice of the angry customer from this morning shouts in your other ear, "Your quality isn't what it needs to be."

Your mother pipes up and says, "Now don't you lie to the nice man across the desk from you."

You blink twice, your eyes avoid the prospect's eyes, and you mumble, "Well, what do you think?"

The prospect replies, "You made some very interesting points. I'm not sure it's quite right for us. Let me think about it and run it by a few of my people. I'll get back to you."

You transmitted your doubt to the prospect. It should be no surprise when you get a Maybe or a No.

People of high integrity have trouble using techniques to sell products they don't believe in.

Not Taking "Maybe" for an Answer

Perhaps you've run across the concept that whatever you believe to be true *is* true, even if it isn't a fact. If you believe that if you don't close, you're a loser, you will have a tendency to accept Maybe for an answer. What if you believed an answer of Maybe was worse than a No? You would act differently.

You know what I mean by a Maybe.

"That was a great presentation, but see me in ninety days."

"We'll keep you in mind."

"I want to think it over."

Accidental Salespeople gladly accept these Maybes and put a positive spin on them back at the office. "She's still very interested and I'm going back in ninety days."

If sales managers would yell and scream about Maybes, their salespeople would get more decisions and more of those decisions would be Yeses.

You've taken the prospect through all sixteen steps in the process and have done a lot of work without getting paid for it. You have sold the prospect on your process. The prospect knows you are making a proposal now and it's time to make a decision.

Producers of infomercials pay for the privilege of making their presentation. They never fail to ask enthusiastically for the order. You too have paid for the privilege of asking for the order with all the work and time you invested. If you've come this far and don't ask, you should feel very bad.

If you ask and don't get the order and get a Maybe, you should feel horrible. If you ask and get a No, you should be glad that you got a decision and focus on the fact that you have nine other prospects in process. If you get a Yes, you should feel great and use that momentum.

At this step a stall or "continuation" is unacceptable. You need to get a decision. If you can't get a decision, you deserve information about why you can't get it. And if you can't get that, you can fall back to getting a date on which the decision will be made.

You might say to the prospect, "I would rather have you tell me No right now than Maybe." Then review the steps you've taken and the benefits of the plan. The prospect has time invested in this sale too. Putting off a decision wastes both your time and hers. You've done a lot of work to earn the business. Use what you've done to make the sale.

"May I make a suggestion? If you are trying to let me down easy, I'd prefer to terminate this process now. I'd suggest at the very minimum our next step would be to present this to the full committee with your endorsement and me present. Is that feasible?"

Always ask the prospect to take the next step in your process with you. (You have been asking all the way through the process.) The fact that you ask for the order should not come as a great surprise, nor should it come out of the blue.

I've heard all the tricky, manipulative closes. So have your customers. The No that means Yes close has been around for so long I forgot who I stole it from. The rationale behind it is that it is easier for people to say No than Yes.

When you ask for the order, you want the order, or you want specific information that will help you adjust your proposal so that you can get the order. "Is there any reason why we can't go ahead with this proposal?" is a question that will elicit either a No—which means the prospect is now a customer—or a Yes, in which case you should get a specific objection that you can handle. After you deal with the objection, ask again. "Now is there any reason we can't do business?"

"No."

"Thank you. Please sign here."

Objection Prevention and Handling

Now we're going to deal with objection prevention and objection handling. Objections occur not just at the end of your presentation, but throughout the selling process. Prospects object to meeting with you, to revealing vital information about their problems, to your price, and even to taking action.

Objection prevention may be a more important skill than objection handling. Dale Carnegie said it this way: "The best way to win an argument is to avoid it."

Famed golf pro the late Harvey Penick told the story about a student who came to him for a lesson to help him get out of sand traps. Penick recommended that he first take a lesson on how to keep the ball on the fairway.

Prevent as many objections as you can. Handling objections is a must-have selling skill. "Resistance is the reason for the existence of salespeople," the saying goes. At the same time, you shouldn't have to fight your way to every sale.

Seven Ways You Can Prevent Rejection and Objections

1. *Work on your beliefs about selling and rejection—Put your systems on the line.* If you believe that you are putting your **self** on the line every day in selling, then rejection may hurt you more than it should.

Here's a slightly different way to think about selling. Don't put yourself on the line; put your proposal on the line, or rather on the table. There's a big difference.

Sure, you've got to have a strong ego drive to make sales. You've got to want to succeed. But you don't have to take every No as a personal affront. They are saying No to your proposal, not to you.

Earlier in this book I described a nine-step appointment-getting system. In Step 1, I recommended sending prospects an article about an issue or trend in their industry along with a business card. The first contact is not even live. It is a business card attached to an article with a brief note, "Thought you might be interested in this," written right on the business card. The next step is to send another article, and then a couple of days later send the letter.

You've discovered that sending a couple of articles, the letter, and following up with a telephone call dramatically increases the number of calls taken and appointments booked. Using a system like this prevents some rejection.

If after sending a couple of articles and the letter, the prospect still doesn't want to meet with you the prospect hasn't rejected you; he's rejected your appointment-getting system. You haven't put yourself on the line; you've put your appointment-getting system on the line. You don't have to say **you** got rejected. You can say instead this system worked 40 percent of the time. You can either accept a 40 percent closing ratio or work to improve the system.

You aren't putting your **self** on the line. You're putting your systems on the line. And you can always improve your systems.

Of course, the only way you can blame your system is to have one. Systematizing your approach to selling is part of building your money machine. Learning to realistically label what happens to you is a powerful rejection-prevention strategy.

Instead of saying, "I blew that proposal," say, "He rejected my proposal, not me. I worked for three hours putting it together. I learned what he doesn't like and I can re-present in three weeks."

2. *Control what you ask for—especially early in the process.* Don't try to go too far, too fast. On the first phone call or the first cold contact, you are selling the prospect on meeting with you, not on buying your product or service.

One script that has worked well for many salespeople is this: "I don't know if you should be using my product or not. That's why the first meeting we have is a non-decision-making, fact-finding call."

The purpose of this script is to reduce the tension in your prospect and to advance the process to the next level. It's much better than the trite, "Your account has just been assigned to me, and I want to learn a little about your business so I can help you." There's a big difference in the way you'll be perceived and received.

3. *Do not ask for an appointment with the new prospect this afternoon or tomorrow morning.* Remember to ask the prospect for the appointment next week. It's much easier to schedule you into a blank calendar than into an already crazy schedule. It also appears, if you've asked for the appointment next week, that you are not desperate for the meeting.

If you **are** desperate for the meeting, it is even more important that you appear not to be desperate for the meeting.

Remember: Think of selling as a series of advances—little closes that lead to the order. Before every call, think about how you are going to advance the sale. Also think about your fall-back position if the prospect says No to your first suggestion.

4. *Use the Magic Phrase: "This is the way I work."* Tell the prospect how you work and what is going to happen so that she doesn't have to defend against your sales tactics.

Get the prospect to buy the way you sell first, before you try to sell your product or service. For one thing, selling the prospect on the way you sell is an easier sale to close. And for another, it sets up the rest of the call. Use the phrase, "This is the way I work," and then lay out the steps in your sales process and the work you propose to do to earn the prospect's business.

5. *Get in the last word.* Sales is a series of defeats punctuated by profitable victories. You are not going to win them all. But when you lose, you have the right to politely voice your opinion.

I have said things like this:

"I worked very hard on this presentation in order to earn your business, and I'm sorry you didn't decide to go with this plan. But I do appreciate the fact that you told me No instead of Maybe. I once read that great salespeople take rejection as information instead of taking it personally. What could I have done differently on this proposal?"

Or you might say something like this:

"John, I've made three presentations to you, and we've had twelve meetings together, and you have yet to purchase anything from me. I'm going to give you a three-month hiatus. I'm not giving up. I'm just going to retool my approach and see if we can come at this in a different way. Fair enough? In the meantime, I'm going to need some other people to meet with. May I ask you for a referral of a businessperson I might be able to help?"

This is a form of giving up without giving up. When you offer to go on hiatus, the prospect may tell you what's really keeping you two from doing business. At the very worst, you'll get some decent referrals. You've taken control of a situation that wasn't going anywhere anyway.

6. *Work by referrals.* Always ask your prospects if you can use their names as a reference. Ask them if they know someone they feel you could help. Ask them about a specific prospect on your list that you are having trouble with. Ask them, occasionally, if they would make a call or send a letter on your behalf.

7. *Drop names of successful clients you work with when talking to a new prospect.* Don't overdo it, but understand that prospects want to know you have helped others. If you're brand new to the industry, discuss your other sales experiences and your education and how that has prepared you to help the prospect.

The point is you should be sharing information instead of pitching product. Share information with prospects about business issues, trends in their own industry, and yes, even your own background.

You are not a machine. You have feelings that can be hurt and beliefs that can be shaken. But you are building a money machine and systematizing much of your selling process. You are not putting yourself on the line. You are putting your systems on the line. And you can always improve your systems.

Strategies for Handling Objections

You prevent objections by preparing for your call, by qualifying prospects better, and by demonstrating that you understand the prospect's business and needs before presenting your solution.

Going through your selling process and telling the client what is going to happen heads off a lot of objections. Still, some prospects will object to meeting with you. Some prospects will object to your price. Some prospects will object because they don't see any need for your product. You need strategies for handling the objections that you can't (or didn't) prevent.

1. *Don't answer the first objection.* Most first objections aren't substantial enough even to deal with. Prospects give you their standard objection that gets rid of most salespeople. "I want to think it over," "Your price is too high," "We had a bad experience with your company," "I don't have enough time to meet with you," etc. You can't "handle" these objections until you quantify or qualify them. Therefore, you need to be very conscious of strategy #2.

2. *Reverse all objections.* Reversing simply means giving the objection back to the prospect to expand upon. The prospect says, "Your price is too high." You say, "When you say our price is too high, that means . . . ?" Reversing is a powerful strategy espoused by the late sales trainer David Sandler. Reversing should get you enough information so you can deal with a true objection. Example: "Your competitor is only charging $172,000, and you're asking $195,000." Now you know you're $23,000 apart, and you can sell the prospect on why your proposal is worth $23,000 more.

3. *Count to three before answering any objection.* Listen carefully and consider what the prospect is saying before you jump in with your side of the story. As you may have guessed, your silence might also act as a kind of reverse. If you don't answer the objection right away, the prospect may feel compelled to add critical information.

4. *Agree with the objection and use the energy behind it.* Agreeing with the objection is one of the most underutilized but most powerful strategies available to you. Finding something you and the prospect can agree on actually builds rapport. Tapping into the prospect's feelings and not just the prospect's words helps you determine just how important the objection is. Here's an example:

"Your price is ridiculous!"

"We have the highest priced widget on the market today. You're absolutely right. You sound angry about that." (Listen.)

Oftentimes the prospect will say something like, "I'm not angry. You have a right to charge whatever you want to charge."

You can come back with, "Are you willing to look at how we can ultimately save you money, or is price the only criteria?"

And then you can go into all the things your product does that your competitors' don't.

5. *Agree with the feeling, if not the content.* Sometimes the prospect gives you an objection that's so ill-founded you **can't** agree with it. At that point, you might have to agree with the prospect's feeling instead of the content of the objection.

"Your engineering is subpar."

"I understand how you can feel that way. And at the same time, in the past five years we've completely transformed our engineering department, and the new vice president of engineering has gradually raised the standards, so I can confidently say we're an engineering leader."

Often you're called on to defend the company's honor and make strong statements to refute prospect misinformation or competitors' disinformation. Agreeing with the feeling and acknowledging the prospect's right to have it helps set up your strong rebuttal and makes it less confrontational.

6. *Tell a story.* At this stage of your career you've no doubt heard of the feel-felt-found method of handling objections.

"You know, Mr. Jones, I know how you **feel**. Ed Whitlock

over at Acme Widgets **felt** the same way. But when Acme's people implemented our system, they **found** huge cost-reduction benefits and increased reliability."

This is a very formulaic approach. Your job is to tell a story about a client who is benefiting from the same product or service your prospect objects to, and to package that story in such a way that it reaches the prospect emotionally and logically and eliminates the objection.

Story selling is a powerful tool that bypasses arguments by using a third party to whom all the benefits have already accrued. The prospect can't argue with the success of one of your happy clients. That's why stories are so powerful.

7. *Express curiosity or interest.* Sometimes an objection is so off-the-wall that it surprises you, because you've never heard it before. In that case, honesty is the best policy.

"Really? You're the first person who's ever complained about slow delivery times. I'm curious. Where did that idea come from?"

As you can see, this is a kind of reverse, but your incredulity should be honest and not feigned. In cases like this, truth is better than creativity.

8. *Confront with the brutal truth.* "See me in ninety days," the prospect says.

"John, it's been my experience that as soon as I walk out the door, you will quit thinking about my proposal. Usually 'See me in ninety days' means there's a part of my proposal I haven't handled well. What is your main concern with what I've presented, and what has to change in ninety days for us to do business?"

9. *Give the panic button answer.* Finally, it's a good idea to memorize the panic button answer to any objection a prospect could think of. The panic button answer is, "I understand (pause), and at the same time . . ." Here's an example:

Objection: "I had a bad experience with your company."

Answer: "I understand. And at the same time, time passes and things do change. I mean, I'm new, the district manager's new, and we've made some major improvements in our product line. What will it take to make things right with you and move on?"

Your prospects often object to test your convictions and see what you're made of, not just to blow you off. They challenge you to learn your business and earn their business. You need to rise to that challenge.

An objection is a wonderful thing, because if there were no objections, the **first** salesperson to make the call would make the sale instead of the **best** person making the sale.

As a buyer, I wanted someone to engage me and challenge me to do something different. Your prospects want the same thing from you.

When you control the focus, you control the meeting. What is the prospect's problem that your company, your creativity, your being on the account and adding value can solve? When you focus on helping the prospect get what he wants instead of what you want to sell him, you get fewer objections and make more sales.

Two Powerful Thoughts

Let me leave you with two powerful thoughts that may change your whole philosophy of selling.

You don't have to prove someone wrong for you to be right. That's true because two points of view **can** exist simultaneously.

These two thoughts can make selling less stressful for you and your prospects. Instead of a debate you find **common ground**.

The secret to building rapport with a prospect is to find something you both agree on and build from there instead of debating insignificant things.

Life is not a contest.

The best way to handle objections is to prevent them. You do that by thorough preparation, professional questioning, and careful listening. If you answer all your prospect's questions as they arise, your prospect will have no objections to raise. When objections arise, you've got some strategies for handling them. The main strategy is always to get more information before you try to handle an objection.

One of the most important lessons in this book is: You don't have to prove someone wrong in order for you to be right. Two points of view can exist simultaneously. Put aside the need for one-upmanship. Concentrate instead on finding common ground.

Note

1. *Glengarry Glen Ross.* 1992. Directed by James Foley. New Line Cinemas. Videocassette.

Chapter 12

No Dessert until You Finish Your Peas

You don't usually think about all the standards your parents set for you. But chances are the last time you went to an all-you-can-eat buffet, you started at the salad bar instead of the dessert table.

If your parents set standards and defined limits when you were growing up, consider yourself very fortunate indeed.

- No dessert until you finish your peas.
- One-half hour of television per night **after** you've finished your homework.
- In bed with the lights out at nine o'clock sharp on school nights.

Parents inevitably put up with a lot of whining as their children test their resolve and try to extend the limits.

"You're too strict."

"But, Mom, everybody's parents let them stay out until midnight."

"I didn't ask to be born."

Great parents set standards and hold their children accountable. When their kids grow up they have more self-discipline. They can "self-manage."

Self-management is critical to sales success.

One of the great things about selling is the tremendous amount of freedom it affords. Your boss isn't constantly looking over your shoulder. Also, one of the **worst** things about selling is the tremendous amount of freedom it affords you. Take your choice.

For undisciplined salespeople with lax standards, this freedom is a recipe for disaster. They can drive around aimlessly passing prospect after prospect. Sometimes you can find them purposefully driving golf balls at the range. (Just because you're wearing a pager doesn't mean you're at work.)

Children learn just how much they can get away with before parents intervene. Discipline can be as mild as a stern look or a "time-out." Discipline can escalate to loss of privileges and being "grounded." Parents discipline you so that, ultimately, you behave in a disciplined way all by yourself.

Your company probably sets certain performance standards for you. A standard is a measurable indicator of performance, often involving a consequence. If you don't work to a certain standard, there are extra meetings for you, coaching, pleading, and finally termination.

Many salespeople try to test the limits their managers will tolerate. They turn in their call reports a couple of days late, knock off early on Friday afternoons, and save most of their creativity for their sales reports.

And at the same time, many companies have wishes instead of standards. Without standards there is no discipline.

When Accidental Sales Managers complain about the lack of effort on behalf of their salespeople, it often sounds like this:

"I wish my people would get to work on time."
"I wish my people would write better proposals."
"I wish my people would make more calls."

Let's define self-management as performing enough steps in your selling process every day, week, and month at a high enough quality in order to deny yourself the unpleasant opportunity of failing or getting fired. Setting higher standards than your company sets for you is one way to surpass old limits you placed on yourself.

Accidental Salesperson Axiom:
Your objective isn't to set high standards
for yourself and your sales career.

Corollary:
You set high standards
so that you can achieve your objectives.

An objective or goal is what you want to happen at a certain time. "On May 31, two years from now, I will have booked an additional $1,200,000 in new business."

Few sales books fail to tell you the importance of setting goals. Yet many unsuccessful salespeople have very high goals. Setting goals alone isn't the answer. So what's the missing ingredient?

Setting higher **performance standards** is the key to helping you achieve your higher goals.

Think of it this way. The goal is the "what." The standards are the "how."

Let's discover how standards and objectives work together. I'll start with a story.

There are breaks at my seminars, but I rarely get to take one. Someone always wants to talk about something. At a seminar at Barren River State Park Lodge near Glasgow, Kentucky, one of the participants approached me during the morning break. I recognized Connie from the year before. She shook my hand and then put her left hand on my right hand and held it there for a long time. She looked into my eyes and said, "Chris (it sounded like Chree-us), after your seminar last year I increased my sales by $7,000! Thank you."

She actually sounded excited about a number that didn't do much for me.

"That's nice, Connie," I said without much enthusiasm.

"Seven thousand dollars a month," she added.

I squeezed her hand a little harder, shook it enthusiastically, and said, "That's very good. Congratulations!"

She just smiled and said, "In Pikeville, Kentucky, that's a miracle."

It does sometimes seem miraculous how much more money your prospects can come up with when you align your behavior with the things they value. However, these kinds of stories happen so often to our students that we no longer label them miraculous.

Here is a simple exercise you can do to see exactly how objectives and standards work together. It require seven minutes of silence on your part and a little bit of thinking and note taking. These will be the most profitable seven minutes you can spend today, so do it now.

Pick a number that represents a significant increase in your sales. Connie thought $7,000 a month was a miracle. Pick your own number and your own time frame. You may want to consider an entire quarter or even a full year.

Enter the number on the worksheet below or on a blank sheet of paper. Then make a list of twenty things that would have to happen for you to increase your sales by that number and in the time frame you've indicated. By listing twenty ideas instead of two or three, you are telling your brain to go to work for you and to think beyond the obvious and easy answers. Please do this little exercise now and we'll work with your list once you have it completed.

What would have to happen for me to increase my sales by _____ per _____?

1. _____
2. _____
3. _____
4. _____
5. _____
6. _____

7. _____
8. _____
9. _____
10. _____
11. _____
12. _____
13. _____
14. _____
15. _____
16. _____
17. _____
18. _____
19. _____
20. _____

You have just started the process of setting higher standards for yourself.

In order to achieve the bigger dollar figure, you have to set higher standards. You have your new objective—the dollar figure you want to achieve. And you have a list of things that need to happen in order for you to achieve it. Many of the things on your list involve higher standards of performance than you're accomplishing now. You will have to hold yourself to these higher standards in order to accomplish the stretch goal.

Thousands of people have completed this exercise in my seminars. The first question I ask after giving them seven minutes of silence is, "What was that exercise like for you?" There have been a variety of answers.

One participant raised his hand and said, "I now see exactly what I need to do to get better. If you had told me I needed to do these things, I would have resisted. But when I wrote them down, they meant more to me."

"I now realize that I have more control over my sales than I thought I did," said another salesperson.

"I'm mad," said a third one. "If I had been doing the

things I already know I need to do, I would have been making more money all along."

So you now have an objective and a list of twenty ideas to help you achieve that objective. You're off to a good start, but the chances are good that your standards aren't quite up to my standards for **writing** standards just yet.

Let's work with the list you created to make sure you have measurable indicators of performance. Let me guess at a few of the things you wrote down. A typical list looks like this the first time through:

1. Get better organized.
2. Do more prospecting.
3. Ask for more referrals.
4. Write better proposals.
5. Ask for more money.

Very noble, but hardly measurable. If your list looks like this and if you stop there, you will be like most Accidental Sales-people. They have a vague idea that they should be doing more than they are and doing it better. They just never define what "more" means and what "better" looks like. They have frail wishes instead of solid standards.

"No dessert until you finish your peas" is a standard.

"Get better organized" will be a wish unless and until you can tell when you become better organized. Having a standard for being organized will also let you know exactly what you need to do when you are disorganized. In order to make this "Get better organized" a measurable indicator of performance you need to rewrite it as a quality, quantity, timeliness, and/or cost standard. What would getting better organized look like if you actually got better organized? Here are some possibilities:

- Take fifteen minutes to plan and prioritize my to-do list. (Timeliness standard)
- Keep one project on my desk at a time. (Quantity standard)
- Schedule a one-hour appointment with myself daily to work on A1 priority. (Quality and Timeliness standards)

- Invest $1,500 in a new laptop computer and a sales-tracking software program, and have it up and running in sixty days. (Cost and Quality standards)

At the end of the day, you can measure whether you worked to those standards or not (see Figure 12-1). If you did, you are better organized and you know why. If you only took ten minutes to plan, there is a gap between the standard you set for yourself and your actual performance. If there are piles of paper on your desk instead of one project, you are not working to the standard.

The concept of "closing the gap" between the standard and your actual performance is what gives standards their power. Think of it this way. If your actual performance falls short of the standard, you have a gap. Your standard is fifteen minutes of planning, and for three days, your actual performance has fallen short. You have a gap. By closing the gap, you will get your performance back on track, or back to the standard you set for yourself.

Self-managers understand the power of managing the gap and not the goal. They set higher goals and hold themselves to higher standards. Set the goal, and then set the stan-

Figure 12-1. Gap management is something you can do so your sales manager doesn't have to.

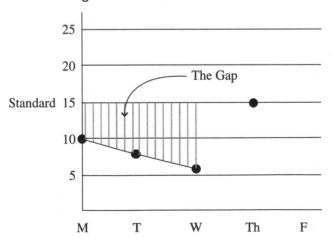

dards that will help you reach your goal. Let's convert one other wish into a measurable standard of performance.

"Do more prospecting" is a wish.

"Send out ten seeds per week" is a standard. You can check off when you do it. You can graph it. You know when you don't do it. You feel terribly guilty about it and close the gap.

Accidental Salespeople don't understand how much control they have in sales and therefore don't take control of their careers. When you are selling on purpose you start to focus on performance and not just sales. If you follow sports and read about your favorite team in the newspapers, you've seen box scores. Box scores give you the details of how the final score was put on the board. To true fans, the **how** is far more interesting than the **what** (the final score). Managers use the information from the box scores to plot their strategies for the next game. It's the analysis of the "game within the game" that yields usable information, not the final score.

Great salespeople understand the game within the game. They don't sell by accident. They analyze every move they make carefully. Their standards allow them to achieve their objectives. They are always on the lookout for something they can do to gain control of the sales process.

Accidental Salespeople sense they need to be doing more, but are not specific about what "more" means. They want to do "better," but lack the quality standards that let them know when they actually are doing better. The Proposal-Writing Template may help you do more with less. Many salespeople have discovered that they can sell more by making five Level 2 presentations than they can by making ten Level 1 presentations. Working to specific standards doesn't necessarily mean working longer and harder.

Look at the list of twenty items you created. Go through it and pick the five best ideas for achieving your new objective. Now convert those five ideas into standards. Make them measurable indicators of your performance by adding a quality, quantity, timeliness, and/or cost component. All that is left is to commit yourself to tracking your performance and holding yourself accountable to those standards. Keep track of your performance daily, weekly, and monthly. If you start to fall below the standard, close the gap quickly.

"Shovel the piles when they are small" is the best advice for Accidental Salespeople who have decided to hold themselves to a higher standard. Don't wait until your actual performance gets so far below your standard that you can't get it back up without extreme effort. For example, let's say you set a standard to write three (quantity) Level 2 (quality) proposals per week but only manage to write two of them this week. Close the gap next week by writing four proposals. If you only write two proposals two weeks in a row, you'll need to write five proposals the third week. Now you've got a big pile of work to do. Close the gap when it is small.

If you want to achieve your objectives without kissing your home life good-bye, you need to grasp how objectives and standards work together. For too many Accidental Salespeople, the only answer they can come up with is to work harder and longer in order to sell more. Since they are already working longer and harder than they ever thought they would, they become discouraged.

You are going to do it differently. You are going to increase your sales by doing everything better. You are already seeing that you can get more out of every single prospect interaction by simply choosing to approach your prospects at Level 2 and by having more Level 3 and 4 "moments" and including Level 3 and 4 pages in your proposals.

Holding yourself to higher standards is the final refinement.

To help you get off to a fast start with standard setting, use the list of standards on the next page, you might want to consider adapting. Each standard contains a blank that you fill in so that it is your number and reflects your reality.

Start with just three to five standards the first week. When your actual performance meets or exceeds the standard, you can adjust the standard upward and/or add a new standard or two. Don't go overboard and hold yourself to twenty-five or fifty standards. Someday you may have ten or fifteen standards in place. If you are already doing things on this list habitually, keep doing them and add standards that will help you achieve your objectives.

Suggested Standards for Accidental Salespeople who have chosen to sell on purpose:

- Take _____ minutes to plan each day and prioritize my action list.

- Ask _____ customers per _____ for a referral.

- Get into position to ask prospects for $_____ per _____.

- Have _____ (qty) prospects in process and track them on my _____ (qty) Most Wanted List.

- Make a minimum of _____ new business moves weekly. (Each time you move one prospect one step in your process, it counts as one new business move.)

- Write a minimum of _____ Level _____ proposals per _____.

- Attend _____ sales seminar(s) or personal improvement program(s) per _____.

- Send _____ articles (seeds) per _____ to prospects.

- Send _____ articles per _____ to current customers.

- Read for _____ minutes/hour(s) per _____ in my field to become an expert.

- Dial the phone a minimum of _____ times per _____.

- Wash my car _____ per _____.

- Shine my shoes _____ per _____.

- Rehearse any presentation for more than $_____ with my sales manager

- Arrive _____ minutes before any firm appointment with a prospect or customer.

- Return phone calls within _____ minutes/hour(s) of receiving them.

- Write down everything I promise or tell a prospect or customer I am going to do and act on that promise.

- Convert a Customer Needs Analysis meeting into a written proposal within _____ business days.

- Book the proposal before leaving the needs analysis meeting.

This certainly is not meant to be an exhaustive list—nor is every standard appropriate for every company or salesperson. It's merely meant to get you past the "make more calls" mentality. Your standards will be better than mine precisely because they are your standards.

Start with the objective and then write your standards. You will immediately gain control by choosing to change your focus. When you quit focusing on sales and start measuring the performance that leads to sales, you are selling on purpose. The disciplined approach to selling will earn you new respect and a lot more money. And there's an added benefit.

Your parents will be so proud of you.

Chapter 13

Service Is Not Something You Do When You're Too Tired to Sell

Many salespeople don't think in terms of "closing" sales anymore. They think of opening a relationship. Since your best customers are also your best prospects for other products and future renewals, consider having a service process much like the sales process you've been working through to the close (or open).

Customer service is given plenty of lip service today. But servicing the account may mean anything you did when you were too tired to sell anybody else.

All salespeople are also buyers. We buy all kinds of things. I buy a lot of airline tickets. I wrote parts of this book during an around-the-world speaking tour that included stops in Sydney, Australia; Auckland and Rotorua, New Zealand; Berlin, Germany; and in Brighton, Oxford, Maidstone, and Manchester, England. Thirty-five days and more than 25,000 miles in the air.

Here's the discovery I made on that trip: I hate flying.

At the same time, I love to be upgraded.

On the ten-and-a-half-hour leg from Bangkok to Frankfurt, the Thai Air reservationist moved me from Business Class to First Class. I still wear the pajamas they gave me and tell everyone about the full reclining seats and how little jet lag you get when you sleep through the night.

Years before, I was returning from an easy nine-day trip. The flight attendant came up to me and said, "Mr. Little, what would you like for dinner once we are airborne?"

"It's Lytle," I gently corrected her, stressing the long "i" sound.

"Oh, I'm terribly sorry."

"That's okay. It happens all the time."

"But Mr. Lytle, you are a 100K Premier Executive, one of our very best customers, and I want to get your name right."

"Well, thank you."

Now, I know that this flight attendant had never seen me before and would likely never see me again. And I knew that she knew my name because of the printout that the gate agent gave her. And I knew that the frequent flyer status is on that sheet because of the computer.

But I didn't care.

It's nice to be recognized as an important customer and called by name.

Just before we landed, the flight attendant came back and whispered something in my ear. "Do you like wine?"

"Why, yes I do."

"We have a bottle of Chardonnay left over." She opened the overhead bin. "Is this your suitcase?"

"Yes."

She opened my suitcase and carefully placed the bottle of wine inside. "I just saw how many cities you've been to on this trip and how many United legs you've taken. Thanks for flying United, Mr. Lytle."

"You're welcome, and thank you."

Sarah was waiting for me at Baggage Claim when I got home.

"Hi, honey. How was your trip?"

I unzipped my suitcase and grasped the neck of the bottle and held it up like it was some kind of trophy. "They gave me a bottle of wine," I said grinning. United Airlines **noticed** me!"

The airlines define a "frequent flyer" as someone who

takes three round trips a year. You can see why they try to build loyalty with frequent flyers like me. If United loses me, they need about twenty frequent flyers to make up for my volume and mileage.

They know it. **You** need to know what losing a big customer means to you. How many average customers will it take to make up the difference? Then you can act intelligently and accordingly to build a major customer follow-up program.

Accidental Salesperson Axiom:
Even customers who hate to buy from you
love being recognized as an important customer.

Corollary:
Every customer is silently
(or not so silently) crying, "Notice me!"

To this day, United Airlines gets around 70 percent of my business.

Keeping customers happy is the purpose of the last power tool, "The Customer Service Process." It may be the most important tool in this book since your current customers are your best prospects. It's just that you can't use it until you've "accidentally" sold somebody something. (Just kidding.) You are now selling on purpose and closing more sales. Not losing customers you already have is the final piece of the puzzle.

If you cannot benefit from repeat business, read no further. If, however, your business relies on selling more to the same clients or on forging strong relationships throughout their companies, this is for you.

The Customer Service Checklist

❏ *The Thank You note.* A three-line, handwritten Thank You note has more impact than a computer-generated one. Here's one we might use at The Lytle Organization:

Dear _____,

Thank you for the order you placed today. Our mission is to help transform sales departments into sales forces. Expect your first shipment in two days and a follow-up call from me on Thursday.

Sincerely,

American business (the retail sector, at least) has lost the art of saying "Thank You." Perhaps that's because Captain Kangaroo is not teaching us the two magic words anymore: "Please and Thank You."

"There you go" has replaced "Thank you" in most transactions. However, in Canada, people are so polite they say "Thank you" to automatic banking machines. Usually.

Recently, a Canadian friend of mine told me about an exchange he had had with a retail clerk in suburban Toronto.

"Chris," he said, "I thought I was in the United States. I made a purchase at a store in the mall. The clerk took my money, rang up the sale, put the merchandise in a bag, slid the bag across the counter, and said, 'There you go.'"

My friend Bob Neilson very politely asked, "Aren't you going to say, "Thank You?"

"It's on your receipt, eh?"

Printing "Thank You" on a receipt hardly takes the place of a genuine Thank You. And sending out a computerized letter doesn't take the place of a handwritten Thank You note.

If you have a customer service department to do these things, great. If not, you will have to service what you sell.

Service is not what you do when you are too tired to sell. It is part of the sales process. It can build loyalty, reduce customer churn, and provide opportunities for writing new business.

So put what you've promised in your planner or computer and go to Step 2.

❏ *The follow-up phone call.* You may add additional information or make sure the customer is using the product.

❏ *The clipping service.* Set a goal to provide one Level 3 touch eight or ten times per year. Intermittent articles are better than, say, sending an article every month. You might send the first one three weeks after the order, then two weeks, then five weeks later. The object is to keep your name and the company name before the buyer.

❏ *Social.* Plan a series of breakfasts or lunches with the buyer or end users. Depending on how often you see the customer, breakfasts and lunches help you build relationships and gather more data.

❏ *Get key customers to your facility.*

❏ *Letter from top management.* This can be a form letter but should be personally signed by someone high up in the company. It follows a big order or the one-year anniversary of the first order.

❏ *Follow-up phone call #2.*

❏ *Orchestrate calls from key people in your company.* (Comptroller, Plant engineer, Delivery supervisor)

❏ *Provide a twenty-four-hour hotline for questions or problems.*

❏ *The newsletter.* Information on business issues. This can be a one-page, Level 3 newsletter that goes out to every prospect and client. In it are business quotes, news about Web sites, and information from books and articles you read. This quick-read format is designed to brand you as a source of business expertise and intelligence.

Look at a one-year tracking program for your customer. Count how many touches you actually provide. How much recognition do you give your top clients? A trip to The Masters is unforgettable. If your response is "Forget about that," then a series of personalized touches can help to solidify the relationship.

If you have a service department, you may be doing these things already. The big idea is to put customers into a service process, just like you put prospects into your sales process. They are still hearing from your competitors. They really need to hear from you so they feel important.

Repeat business is profitable business. You already have the relationship, so the selling cycle is shorter. As you might expect, the best training I ever received on how to do great customer service happened quite by accident.

Accidental Service Training Seminar
The Cruise

Sarah and I were on our first Royal Caribbean cruise. We were very excited about it. I read the cruise brochure our travel agent gave us three times. It advertised a fun-filled week.

And the pictures! The brochure had pictures of beautiful people—men and women—in stunning bathing suits, sunning themselves around a crystal clear pool. In the pictures were smooth seas, sunny days, sumptuous midnight buffets, and luxurious ports of call. The brochure sold the experience and helped us visualize and anticipate what was in store for us when we stepped on board the *Sun Viking*.

Except the reality didn't exactly match the brochure.

When we stepped on board the *Sun Viking*, I was expecting a cruise like the ones I had seen in the brochure. It was the same ship all right. And there were the same bathing suits, but they weren't on the same models that were in the brochure. (There are certain people—men and women—who shouldn't wear bikinis.)

And there were **children** in the swimming pool. And you know what children do in swimming pools. No brochure writer would mention it, but I will.

I'll tell you something else. Nobody ever gets seasick reading a brochure. But once you're on the open ocean, it's a different story. The motion of a ship at sea is not something you can practice getting used to. Either you can either handle it or you can't.

In the brochure the people are sun-tanned. In reality, the people on the deck chairs, including Sarah and I, were wedding-dress white, Wisconsin people.

There is nothing like a mai tai in the morning. I mean in the brochure people drink them, right? Wrong. In the brochure, they are props for the models in the beautiful bathing suits.

Now, two hours into the cruise an interesting thing happens. You mix a couple of early-in-the-day drinks with four hours in the subtropical sun and the undulating motion of the ship and you realize on the first day of the cruise—this isn't what I was expecting!

It's hard to eat a scrumptious dinner while in a seasick-hungover-sunburned state. You can't eat all you can eat when you feel as bad as you've ever felt.

Six days to go.

On the second day it was cloudy. They don't show clouds in cruise brochures. But that was okay. We didn't need any more sun.

Things got better eventually and we enjoyed our new friends and some of the ports we visited.

Still, I remember thinking how I probably wouldn't take another cruise any time soon. On the next to the last day, the cruise director organized a meeting of all first-time cruisers.

"It's time to evaluate your first Royal Caribbean cruise," announced the cruise director. "Our staff members are passing out the evaluation forms for you. But before you fill them out, I'd like to go through each part of the evaluation with you."

The cruise director on the *Sun Viking* had a very important job: to manage the experience of the cruisers—first-time cruisers especially.

He did one of the best postselling jobs at the end of the cruise I have ever seen.

"Now the first thing we're going to rate is the entertainment. Before you make your evaluation, I want to review the week with you. Did all of you see the comedian at the late night show?"

About half the room clapped and I turned to Sarah and smiled, remembering how funny he had been.

"And every night we have had a Las Vegas style show. Remember the magician? How about the Broadway style dance review?"

More applause.

"When we stop at a port, these entertainers get off and meet or are flown to other ships. That way you get a new show every night. It means that whatever Royal Caribbean cruise you take, you'll get great entertainment. Now, folks, please rate us on the entertainment."

Sarah and I circled the highest rating.

"Another thing we want you to rate is the bar service. On Royal Caribbean we do not push drinks, but we want them to be available when you want them. Our standard is ninety-second service. And to do this we have a lot of servers and a host of bartenders. The drinks aren't free, because not everyone wants to drink, so that keeps the cruise price down. But our goal is to charge what you'd pay in a local tavern and not an expensive hotel. Before you rate our bar service, I'd like to ask our entire bar-tending and serving crew to come in. Please give them a round of applause."

Wild, enthusiastic applause.

"Now I'd like you to rate our cabin steward service. Our goal is to service your cabin and never disturb you. So we'll never knock on your door and disturb you to clean your cabin. But we know when you're not in there. How do we know? It's a Royal Caribbean secret. But we know. So whenever you leave, our cabin steward is in there tidying up. That's why you always have clean towels. That's why your shoes are always stowed under your bed and your bed is always made. When you come back, everything is neat and tidy. Shipshape. Ladies and

gentleman, the Royal Caribbean cabin crew. Please give
them a hand and write down your rating.''

You have probably guessed by now that, despite
my early impressions of cruising, I gave Royal Caribbean
excellent ratings and have returned for another cruise.
But I doubt that I would have, had our cruise director
not shown the work that had been done behind the
scenes.

People don't know what you're doing for them unless
you tell them. Find a way to share the behind-the-scenes information.

Cruise companies can't control the weather or the seas,
so they control as much of the experience as they can and tell
you exactly what they are doing to make your experience the
best it can possibly be.

What about you? You're not just a salesperson; you're a
cruise director. You're managing the expectations of your clients and not just making sales. If you want something that
you do to be more valuable, you need to tell your clients what
you're doing.

Selling is teaching. Teaching is selling.

Teach your clients what you do for them that no one else
is doing and good things happen. You get customers who are
more loyal to you and customers who are willing to pay more
for what you're selling, because they now know all the work
that goes into what you're selling.

Back before calculators, we had to learn long division. If
we showed our work, we got partial credit for our effort even
if we didn't come up with the right answer. Show your work
to the customer and you'll get the benefit of the doubt when
something doesn't go completely right.

Speaking of things not going completely right, here are my
Seven Laws of Selling with E-Mail. While I have closed business with e-mail, the reality is that you're better off using
e-mail to book meetings and confirm appointments.

Lytle's Seven Laws of Selling with E-Mail

Lytle Law #1: Do not send more than three simple sentences. A two-sentence e-mail is better. One sentence is best. A typical e-mail from me might read, "Jim, Meeting with client in Twin Cities early Friday morning. Are you free for lunch? Chris." It doesn't matter to Jim whom I'm meeting with, and it doesn't make sense to ask him if he's going to be in town on Friday. He can read my message in seconds and respond in seconds. If he responds "Yes," then we can hammer out the time and place for lunch by e-mail or voice mail. Bottom line: I get two meetings out of one trip and get face-to-face with an important state association executive.

Lytle Law #1A: Use e-mail to book live appointments and phone appointments. "Ed, can you take my phone call at 8:30 Tuesday morning?" is something that has worked with prospects who already know me.

Lytle Law #2: Use e-mail to let people know something is coming. "Sue, your customized kit went out today by overnight UPS. Interesting info highlighted for you. Chris."

Lytle Law #3: Don't send everybody everything. I wonder why I have to scroll down a page of e-mail addresses to get a particularly bad joke or a chain letter.

Lytle Law #4: Never send jokes or chain letters to clients or prospects.

Lytle Law #5: If I want to get name awareness, I will sometimes just use the subject line of the e-mail. "Congratulations on your *Radio Ink* cover story. No other message." The client or prospect can read it and delete my message very quickly, but I get name recognition from my e-mail return address and the chance to recognize the prospect who has done something good. Building self-esteem in customers is a subtle sales builder that you should consider doing more of.

Lytle Law #6: E-mail is a great way to say thank you. A handwritten note is better, but e-mail is better than no thank you at all.

Lytle Law #7: Use e-mail to "tease" your upcoming presentations and confirm them. "Laura, In researching your industry, I found an interesting fact that has shaped the presentation I'll be making tomorrow. See you at 8:30. Chris."

If you're selling today without e-mail, I think you're missing a tremendous opportunity to get yourself in front of more clients. In a recent poll, more than 70 percent of teenagers said they'd give up TV before giving up their computers or the Internet. When they get into sales in a few years, these computer-literate rookies will have an unfair advantage over you. So get going.

Conclusion

Working Your Way to Success

"I'm hungry."

"Me too. Let's go to lunch."

"Where do you want to go?"

"I don't know. Where do you want to go?"

"What are you hungry for?"

"A hamburger."

"Okay, let's go to _____." (Please fill in the blank with the first restaurant that comes to mind that sells hamburgers.)

Chances are very good that the first place you thought of was McDonald's. Over the years, McDonald's' advertising has programmed us to think of this company first when we're hungry for a hamburger. Its top-of-the-mind awareness makes it an easy first choice. Sure, people eat hamburgers at Burger King and Wendy's too.

Many times we're not aware the advertising affected us. We get hungry and go to McDonald's. We don't go to McDonald's because of its advertising. We go to McDonald's because we **are** hungry. And the first place we think of to get a hamburger when we are hungry is McDonald's.

Advertising affects your brain. You may not even be conscious of how you have been programmed. Banks are notorious for using this opening statement in their advertising: "The biggest investment most of us will ever make is the one we make in our home." If you've heard that once, you've heard it a thousand times. Even if you're only half listening that statement goes in one ear and lodges somewhere in the brain.

If that is true then it follows that, "The second biggest investment most of us will ever make is the one we make in our automobile." Countless car dealers have used that headline over the years.

Both are false and misleading. The presidents of the banks, the owners of the dealerships, and their advertising agencies should be put in jail. Because of this false advertising, repeated over and over again, people who have a house and a car are programmed to believe that it just doesn't get any better than that.

Let me ask you a question. Where did you get the money to make the down payment on your house? How can you afford to pay your mortgage every month and make the payments on your car? Most of us acquire things by going to work and exchanging our time and talents for money to buy other things. We're going to secure our futures by working our way to success.

Sound familiar?

One more time, then. What's the biggest investment you will ever make? Your career. Say it with me: "The biggest investment I will ever make is the investment I make in my career."

Your career is the money machine that buys the house, pays for the car, funds your retirement, and provides for your children's college education. Take very good care of that investment because, without it, you won't have your other investments very long.

Mitch had figured this out by the end of *City Slickers,* when he said, "I'm not going to quit my job. I'm just going to do it better."

There are three ways to get rich quick in the United States today:

1. You can marry a billionaire. (Love)
2. You can sue a billionaire for divorce. (Litigation)
3. You can win the lottery. (Good luck)

Love, litigation, and lotteries offer great hope and bad odds. I quit gambling several years ago when I heard a comedian in Las Vegas offer this advice. "Remember, folks, it's your money that builds these beautiful hotels. And always remember, the less you bet the more you lose when you finally win."

I'm betting on my career.

Working your way to success offers the best odds for the rest of us to get rich. It's a slow but sure process. The sooner you start the better.

Since the rest of us are going to have to secure our futures by working our way to success, here's one more of my "road maps" to help guide you.

Of course, it's impossible to graph success, but if you could, it would have these three dimensions:

1. Making meaningful money.
2. Enjoying a sense of fulfillment about what you do.
3. Giving your sales career enough time.

1. *Making meaningful money* is the vertical axis.

Meaningful money for most of us means earning more than the median wage from your job in the country in which

Figure 14-1.   Meaningful money.

1998 median annual earnings of full-time wage & salary workers

$70,000	$71,916	Airplane/pilot navigator
60,000	$62,868	Lawyer
	$60,112	Physician
	$59,228	Aerospace engineer
	$53,196	Chemical engineer
50,000	$50,180	Civil engineer
	$47,164	College/university teacher
	$43,836	Computer programmer
40,000		
	$38,168	Firefighter
	$35,432	Elementary school teacher
	$34,476	Real estate sales
	$32,812	Advertising & related sales
30,000	$30,108	Social worker
	$29,224	Painter/sculptor
	$27,196	MEDIAN U.S. WAGE
	$26,936	Welder and cutter
	$22,412	Secretary
20,000	$20,280	Construction laborer
	$19,136	File clerk
	$18,304	Baker
	$15,392	Sales counter clerk
10,000	$10,608	Child care worker
0		

SOURCE: U.S. Department of Labor, Bureau of Labor Statistics, "Usual Weekly Earnings of Wage and Salary Workers," www.bls.gov/news.release/wkyeng.toc.htm (Last modified date 15 April 1999, downloaded 26 April 1999)

you reside. According to the U.S. Commerce Department of Labor, Bureau of Labor Statistics (see Figure 14-1), the median U.S. wage is $27,196. Take out your W2 and plot where you are right now. There are salespeople who make less than a secretary. There are salespeople who make more than the President of the United States. (Babe Ruth was once asked how he could justify the fact that he made more than the President. "I had a better year," was his reply.)

Reality check: You aren't going to get that million-dollar signing bonus from your favorite NFL team. You're not going to play on the PGA Tour or the Senior Tour. You're never going to be a rock star or movie star. Their incomes are not on this chart. This is the scale for the rest of us.

This chart in no way limits your income, however. By definition half the workers in the United States make more than the median income and half make less.

2. *Enjoying a sense of fulfillment about what you do* is the second dimension of success.

It probably won't surprise you to learn that there are Four Levels (Quadrants) of Success (see Figure 14-2).

Quadrant 1. *You feel empty and you're not making meaningful money.* Every successful salesperson you see has spent some time in Quadrant 1. They have felt empty when prospects rejected them. People who are just starting out in sales may think that they'll never get out of Quadrant 1. It doesn't have to be a permanent condition.

Quadrant 2. *You feel empty, but you're making meaningful money.* The lottery winner who joins a support group might also fit in this category. Chris Farley is buried in a cemetery that I often drive by. He made lots of money but battled his own demons in Quadrant 2. I'm not sure where Leona Helmsly is now, but when she served her time in jail for income tax evasion, she also spent time in Quadrant 2.

Quadrant 3. *You feel fulfilled, but you are not making meaningful money.* Maybe money isn't your thing. I consider people who are fulfilled and not making meaningful money as more successful than empty, rich folks. The piano teacher who

Figure 14-2. It is important to set financial goals. Make sure that you also set goals to become fulfilled in the process.

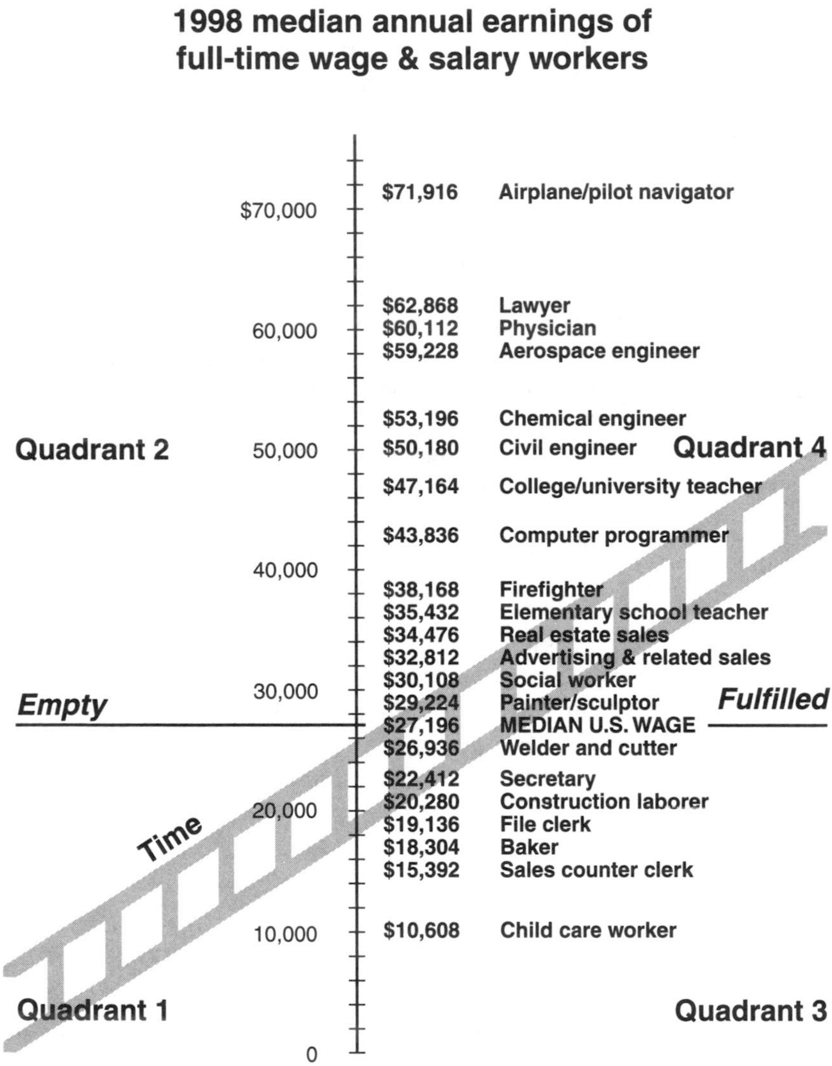

1998 median annual earnings of full-time wage & salary workers

$70,000	$71,916	Airplane/pilot navigator
60,000	$62,868	Lawyer
	$60,112	Physician
	$59,228	Aerospace engineer
	$53,196	Chemical engineer
Quadrant 2 50,000	$50,180	Civil engineer **Quadrant 4**
	$47,164	College/university teacher
	$43,836	Computer programmer
40,000	$38,168	Firefighter
	$35,432	Elementary school teacher
	$34,476	Real estate sales
	$32,812	Advertising & related sales
	$30,108	Social worker
Empty 30,000	$29,224	Painter/sculptor *Fulfilled*
	$27,196	MEDIAN U.S. WAGE
	$26,936	Welder and cutter
	$22,412	Secretary
	$20,280	Construction laborer
Time 20,000	$19,136	File clerk
	$18,304	Baker
	$15,392	Sales counter clerk
10,000	$10,608	Child care worker
Quadrant 1		**Quadrant 3**
0		

SOURCE: U.S. Department of Labor, Bureau of Labor Statistics, "Usual Weekly Earnings of Wage and Salary Workers," www.bls.gov/news.release/wkyeng.toc.htm (Last modified date 15 April 1999, downloaded 26 April 1999)

performs in the local symphony finds fulfillment but may not make the serious money that the guest artist commands. Still, she is doing what she loves to do.

Quadrant 4. *You feel fulfilled and are making meaningful money.* Be careful what you ask for. You might just get it. Setting a goal to make a lot of money without setting a corresponding goal to find fulfillment makes no sense at all once you have a clear vision of what success can be. Ever since I knew it was out there, I've been striving for Quadrant 4 success.

3. *Time* is the third dimension of success and the one that sales managers don't tell you about, especially when they are recruiting you.

It takes time to work your way to Quadrant 4 success. There will be times in sales when you are unfulfilled and not making meaningful money. Giving your sales career enough time is essential. Research by economist Herbert Simon reveals that it takes three to five years to establish yourself in a career and ten years to master it. How many years did Tiger Woods play golf as an amateur before he won The Masters at age twenty-one? How many golf balls did he hit for no money as he worked his way to success?

When times are tough you get through them by focusing on your Quadrant 4 goals. Visualize and feel yourself enjoying the success you've worked so hard to achieve.

People often ask me, "How do you get pumped up for one of your seminars?"

"Coffee and belief" is my standard reply. Believing in what I'm saying is a source of passion. Reading success stories sent in by my students is fulfilling. The fact that they pay helps me maintain my Quadrant 4 position.

One day a woman came up to me before a seminar and said, "Thank you for my career. My company sent me to your seminar last year. I had my resignation letter in my desk drawer, but I figured I'd go get the training and then quit. After your seminar, I had a system for helping my clients. I tore up the letter and I am now very happy and making more money than I believed possible. Thank you for my career."

I spent the money I earned from that seminar many years ago, but I still have the story.

One of my written goals was to write a best-selling self-help book. As I got into this project that goal changed significantly—it evolved. The new goal is to write a book that will resonate with Accidental Salespeople everywhere and make them the "best sellers" in their companies.

If it solves your problem, the money will take care of itself.

My vision is to give you a forum at accidentalsalesperson. com to tell your success stories and to share the refinements you've made with others. Writing a paragraph or a page about what you've done with this material will clarify your thinking while it inspires others. There is a special button on the Web site labeled "Readers Only." It requires a secret password. That password is "Conclusion." It tells us you've read this far and have earned the right to write about your experiences and share what others have written.

When you sell on purpose, you will begin to bring to the table those intangibles that Accidental Salespeople just can't. You have enthusiasm and project confidence. You persist because you believe that what you are doing is right and good.

The challenge is to choose from The Chart the kind of salesperson you are going to be on every client interaction. Everything changes when you make that choice.

Accidental Salesperson Axiom:
Success is not an accident.

Corollary:
Success is a choice.

It was no accident that you picked up this book. You were ready to take your income and your career to the next level. Now you know what the next level looks like and exactly how to get there.

It's been my privilege to help show you the way.

Index